Therefore my he
and my whole be
my flesh also dw

For you will not abandon my soul to
sheol, or let your holy one see corruption.

formatio
TRADITION. EXPERIENCE.
TRANSFORMATION.

Formatio books from InterVarsity Press follow the rich tradition of the church in the journey of spiritual formation. These books are not merely about being informed, but about being transformed by Christ and conformed to his image. Formatio stands in InterVarsity Press's evangelical publishing tradition by integrating God's Word with spiritual practice and by prompting readers to move from inward change to outward witness. InterVarsity Press uses the chambered nautilus for Formatio, a symbol of spiritual formation because of its continual spiral journey outward as it moves from its center. We believe that each of us is made with a deep desire to be in God's presence. Formatio books help us to fulfill our deepest desires and to become our true selves in light of God's grace.

You make known to me the path of life;
in your presence there is fullness of joy;
at your right hand are pleasures
forevermore.   Psalm 16 : 1-11

Also by Dallas Willard:

The Divine Conspiracy

Knowing Christ Today

Hearing God

Renovation of the Heart

The Great Omission

The Spirit of the Disciplines

Also by John Ortberg:

Who Is This Man?

The Me I Want to Be

God Is Closer Than You Think

The Life You've Always Wanted

If You Want to Walk on Water, You've Got to Get Out of the Boat

DALLAS WILLARD

LIVING IN CHRIST'S PRESENCE

FINAL WORDS ON HEAVEN
AND THE KINGDOM OF GOD

WITH A DISCUSSION GUIDE
BY GARY W. MOON

IVP Books

An imprint of InterVarsity Press
Downers Grove, Illinois

InterVarsity Press
P.O. Box 1400, Downers Grove, IL 60515-1426
ivpress.com
email@ivpress.com

InterVarsity Press® is the book-publishing division of InterVarsity Christian Fellowship/USA®, a movement of students and faculty active on campus at hundreds of universities, colleges and schools of nursing in the United States of America, and a member movement of the International Fellowship of Evangelical Students. For information about local and regional activities, visit intervarsity.org.

All Scripture quotations, unless otherwise noted, are from the Holy Bible, New International Version®. NIV®. Copyright© 1973, 1978, 1984 by the International Bible Society. Used by permission of Zondervan Publishing House. All rights reserved.

While all stories in this book are true, some names and identifying information in this book have been changed to protect the privacy of the individuals involved.

Cover design: Cindy Kiple
Interior design: Beth Hagenberg
Images: businessman silhouette: Andrew Penner/Getty Images
         sunset: © Barcin/iStockphoto
         flower: © Steve Bond/Trevillion Images

ISBN 978-0-8308-4633-7 (paperback)
ISBN 978-0-8308-3584-3 (hardcover)
ISBN 978-0-8308-9625-7 (digital)
ISBN 978-8-8308-3585-0 (DVD)

Printed in the United States of America ∞

InterVarsity Press is committed to ecological stewardship and to the conservation of natural resources in all our operations. This book was printed using sustainably sourced paper.

Library of Congress Cataloging-in-Publication Data

Willard, Dallas, 1935-2013.
  Living in Christ's presence : final words on heaven and the kingdom of
God / Dallas Willard and John Ortberg ; with a discussion guide by Gary
W. Moon.
      pages cm
  Includes bibliographical references and index.
  ISBN 978-0-8308-3584-3 (hardcover : alk. paper)
  1. Christian life. I. Title.
  BV4501.3.W54395 2014
  248.4—dc23
                                                                                    2013046579

| P | 22 | 21 | 20 | 19 | 18 | 17 | 16 | 15 | 14 | 13 | 12 | 11 | 10 | 9 | 8 | 7 | 6 | 5 | 4 |
| Y | 35 | 34 | 33 | 32 | 31 | 30 | 29 | 28 | 27 | 26 | 25 | 24 | 23 | 22 | 21 | 20 | 19 |

CONTENTS

PREFACE

Gary W. Moon

I believe that church history will be very kind to Dallas Willard. He lived his life as a rare composite of rigorous academic, passionate Bible expositor and friend of God. Those who knew him well marveled at his mind but loved him because of his firsthand knowledge of God and his desire for others to share his experiences of life in the kingdom.

The book in your hands has been created from the transcript of a conference held February 21–23, 2013, in Santa Barbara, California. The conference was born out of conversations between Dallas and John Ortberg, senior pastor at Menlo Park Presbyterian Church in Menlo Park, California, and a gifted author and speaker.

The primary passion for the conference was to provide an overview of Dallas's writings and ministry—his most impassioned ideas. The conference was built around the theme "Knowing Christ Today" and as a way to present the golden thread that runs through all of his primary writing: that it is possible to know the Trinity intimately and to step into their glorious kingdom.

The talks at the conference by Dallas and John have been edited just a bit to make the transition to create this book, but they retain the conversational feel of a conference. At the start of each chapter of the book is one of the prayers that was prayed during the conference. Each chapter ends with a conversation about the content with further content being drawn out with questions from John to Dallas and from the audience. Also available is a companion DVD of the talks which is taken up along with the book in the discussion guide found in the appendix.

The conference was sponsored by the Martin Institute for Christianity and Culture and the Dallas Willard Center for Christian Spiritual Formation (MIDWC), where I serve as executive director. The MIDWC exists because of the vision and generosity of Eff and Patty Martin. We hope that you find that the book, DVD and discussion guide capture and preserve the nature of the conference—and more importantly, Dallas's thoughts—in a way that will be helpful to you.

1

HOW TO LIVE WELL

Eternal Life Begins Now

Dallas Willard

May you experience grace—God acting in your life, in your thoughts, in your feelings, in your rest. May his face shine upon you. May his shining face lift up over you as you lie down, as you sleep, and give you the thoughts you need to have. The blessing of the Trinity rest upon you and everything you are and do. Let it be so. Amen.

DALLAS WILLARD

W e are on the verge of a time when the church is going to be able to make some decisions. For long periods in the history of the church, as in the history of Israel, there were no significant decisions that could have been made. I think we have been through a pretty tough patch with the church, and I try never to criticize the church, because I know who is in charge of it. But sometimes we need to be conscious of where we are coming from and where we are going.

We are coming into a time when many churches and Christians who are in leadership positions will be able to say it's all about discipleship and transformation into Christlikeness. Now, if you read the New Testament or even the Old Testament, you might have come to that conclusion already. It is hard to avoid, but circumstances in history have a way of claiming us and not letting us see what's actually happening.

We have been through a period when the dominant theology simply had nothing to do with discipleship. It had to do with proper belief, with God seeing to it that individuals didn't go to the bad place, but to the good place. But that developed in such a way that the predominant thought is that a person can have the worst character possible and still get into the good place if he believed the right thing. This disconnection became increasingly burdensome to the church itself until we came to the point that, as is widely discussed, there is not a clear difference between Christians and those who aren't Christians.

Now, that is due partly to the fact that Christian teaching has thoroughly penetrated ordinary society. Many people who are not part of the church and who are not followers of Christ by their own conscious intentions wind up living in a kind of halfway, limp way of living out what Jesus taught and who he was. And it is a familiar fact that the world likes to beat the church with the church's own stick and to criticize it in terms of what Jesus himself taught.

We have perhaps had enough of that, and there are indications that we are ready for a change. That change will make a startling difference in our world, because Jesus' intention for his people from the beginning, and indeed from long before that in God's covenant relationship with the people of Israel, was world revolution. If you read the Great Commission, you may not realize it is about world revolution. If you think it is about planting churches, as important as that may be, if you think it is about evangelization, as that is often understood—no, no, it is about a world revolution promised through Abraham, come to life in Jesus and living on in his people up to today. That is what our hearts hunger for, even when we don't know how to approach it or how to go about it.

KNOWLEDGE OF CHRIST

What I want to talk about is knowledge of Christ today. It is not about faith except insofar as faith is a reflection of knowledge. It is about knowing Christ. One of the things that has happened in the last hundred and a few more years is that society, through its institutions, has very carefully taken Christ's teachings and set them out of the domain of knowledge and put them in an area called faith. That one shift has deprived faith of its power, because faith is never meant to exist apart from knowledge, where knowledge is possible. What is possible through the Scriptures and the actions of God in history is knowledge— knowledge of God, knowledge of human life—and that dignity has to be restored. So our focus is on knowledge for living and the disastrous effects of forcing the teachings of Jesus Christ and his people from the domain of human knowledge.

Now we have an odd thing called secular knowledge. What is that? Is reality secular? If reality is not secular, secular knowledge falls miserably short of what human beings need. Knowledge is what we bring to the world, what pastors and other spokespersons for Christ bring to the world.

Spokespersons for Christ are all men and women, wherever they are, who speak up for Christ and bring knowledge of God. They bring knowledge of the human soul, and without that, the world has no structure. It's all up for grabs, and there are a lot of people grabbing. It is about what you can make out of what you have, rather than how you can come to terms with the realities of God and of his nature and of his purpose in creation and of his sending of Christ and of the coming of the Holy Spirit into the world. They present this as knowledge, and that is the first thing we must understand when we approach the issue of knowing Christ.

The second thing is closely related to it: spokespersons for Christ are those who have knowledge that no one else has. That's why they are the most important people in society. That is because they bring knowledge of what time and eternity are about. They bring knowledge on which people can base their lives. They bring knowledge that can be communicated to others on the basis of experience and reason and Scripture and grace and work and everything else you want to put in the bag.

Spokespersons for Christ have the dignity of bringing that knowledge to everyone around them. One of the sad things is what has happened to witnessing in our culture. Witnessing is not thought of as bringing knowledge, but as attempts to convince people to do things. When you divorce faith from knowledge, you wind up in the position of trying to get people to do things, not of providing them with a basis on which they can then decide how to live and how to lead their lives together. Witnessing has turned into a kind of process of bothering people, and very few people witness because of that.

As a young man, I was a Southern Baptist pastor, and I could very easily inspire guilt in my people by talking about why they didn't witness. This differs a little from denomination to denomination, but that was the sad truth, and I must confess my sin; I often did this because I thought the way to move people was to make them feel, not to provide them with knowledge.

We are here to try to restore the dignity of the spokesperson based on the dignity of the knowledge that they bring. We want to bring forth the people of Christ and let them stand in the world shoulder to shoulder with everyone else who claims to know what they are talking about and to enable individuals to tie into the tradition of Christ and his people, which has always been a tradition of knowledge.

Now, while saying as much as I am, I am probably going to say one or two things that are wrong. You may be getting uneasy, and that is okay. What I say is meant to open things up for discussion. But my main point is that we have to understand the dignity of the knowledge that we possess as followers of Christ.

The famous passage in Hosea 4:6 doesn't say, "My people perish for lack of faith." It says, "My people perish for lack of knowledge." Knowledge and faith are different kinds of things. In my book *Knowing Christ Today,* I describe in depth the difference between faith and knowledge; and while they are both vital, they are different.

SPIRITUAL FORMATION

We dare not take faith out of the area of knowledge. We need to explore not knowledge as such, but the particular knowledge that comes to us in spiritual formation. *Spiritual formation* is an old term. It is new in many circles, but it is as old as the New Testament. The early years of the church were years in which spiritual formation was assiduously studied and developed and written about. If it is at all possible, read the *Philokalia,* one of the earliest collections of Christian writings, or John Cassian's *Institutes,* which are in that same genre. Come to know them to see what spiritual formation is about.

So, what is spiritual formation? It is the process of transforming the person into Christlikeness through transforming the essential parts of the person. Though transforming the mind is absolutely fundamental, the other parts of the self also have to be transformed. Spiritual transformation is not about behavior modification. It is about changing the sources of behavior, so the behavior will take care of itself. When the mind is right and the heart is right and the body and the soul and the relationships that we have in our social world are right, the whole person simply steps into the way of Christ and lives there with joy and strength. It is not a struggle.

One of the lies about the spiritual life is that it is hard. No, no. It is not hard. It is the easy way. What's hard is the other way, and that is what you see when you look at the world. This is a bit of knowledge that we need to bring to people; we need to help them understand that the transformation of the self leads into the life of blessing.

THE EASY YOKE

Consider two passages that are both very familiar. One is in Matthew 11, where Jesus says these words, which are often picked up out of the context, with no question raised about to whom is he speaking: "Come to me, all you who are weary and burdened, and I will give you rest. Take my yoke upon you and learn from me, for I am gentle and humble in heart, and you will find rest for your souls. For my yoke is easy and my burden is light" (Matthew 11:28-30).

The person who has the easiest, the happiest, the strongest life is the person who walks in the yoke with Christ. Only as we do that do we begin to draw the strength and direction that straightens out everything that is wrong in human existence. It does sometimes lead to a battle with a world gone wrong around us, but that world needs that battle, and they need us to stand steady in the easy yoke with Christ.

What is the yoke of Christ? Well, this language referred to oxen in Jesus' day, and it can refer to horses or other animals. It speaks of two animals being yoked together to pull a load. To be in the yoke with Christ is to pull his load with him. What is his load? It is to bring the reign of God into ordinary human life. That is why he came the way he did, lived the way he did and died the way he did. In the midst of a world of ordinary human life he was pulling the load of bringing the kingdom of God into ordinary human life. That was his message. And his message was to everyone.

Rethink your thinking. Repent, as Jesus commanded in Matthew 4:17. *Repent* just means to turn back on how you are thinking about things and to reconsider. Repent, for the kingdom of the heavens is now available to you. That was his message, and if we are going to walk in the easy yoke with Jesus and have the light load that he gives—not light inherently, but light because of who we are yoked to—we need to understand that we are working with the kingdom of God. We are working with the kingdom of the heavens.

Who do you think Jesus is speaking to here? You might say, "Well, anyone who is weary and heavy laden." But we need to put the passage in its context. Jesus had come into a period when he was facing great opposition, great rejection. When you go back and read the whole eleventh chapter of Matthew, you can see that emerging. Even John is questioning Jesus, because Jesus is not living up to his expectations. I heard a person once say, very profoundly, that if you follow Jesus long enough, he will disappoint you. And that is what's going on.

Jesus had been run out of his hometown, Nazareth, and he had moved on to Capernaum and a lot of little cities around there—Chorazin, Bethsaida and some others. He was rejected even though he did wonderful things in their streets. He was rejected because of a prevailing view of religion and God in that society. And so leading up to his words "Come to me, all you that are weary and are carrying heavy burdens," is Jesus' statement, "I thank you, Father, . . . because you have hidden these things from the wise and the intelligent and have revealed them to infants" (Matthew 11:25, 28 NRSV).

He is actually talking to people who are carrying a terrible religious burden. That is what religion does to you. It wears you out. If there is anything that we need to do, it is to learn how to lay down the burdens of religion in a loving, intelligent way.

Let me tell you something that is striking; that is, when you come to spiritual formation, it makes very little difference what your religious position is. No matter what denomination or Christian group you look at, you see that they don't share the same theology. Now, they have to believe certain things about Jesus, but spiritual formation doesn't run with the orthodoxy of a position. Jesus is saying, "Take my yoke." Take the yoke of official religion off your neck. Then you can go back and redeem that, but first you have to learn from him how to live in the yoke of the kingdom of God.

I am not one who thinks that we ought to criticize the church very much. There is nothing wrong with the church that disci- pleship will not cure. Nothing. When you find problems in the church—and this is constantly discussed over and over in the best periodicals, secular and sacred—it is always a lack of dis- cipleship that led to it. It doesn't much matter what the official structure is—whether it is big or little or whatever. What matters is, are you a disciple?

LEADING OTHERS INTO DISCIPLESHIP

It is to a group of disciples that we now turn in the second passage, right at the end of the Gospel of Matthew (Matthew 28:18-20). It is called the Great Commission, but when you look at it closely, you might want to call it the Great Omission, because what Jesus said to do here is rarely done.

Here is what Jesus is saying: I have been given say over everything in heaven and on earth. As you go, make disciples. Immerse them together in the presence of the Trinity, the Father, the Son, and the Holy Spirit. Yes, baptize them in the name, but, dear friends, that doesn't just mean getting them wet while you say those names. It means to immerse them in the Reality. After you have done that, teach them in a way that they actually do what Jesus said. That is the process of spiritual formation. And what comes out at the end is the joy of living in the easy yoke, for you find that to do what Jesus said is the easy and strong way to live forever and in time.

Look at those passages again. First of all, Jesus said, "I have been given all authority." In other words, "I have been given say over everything." We are not sent out without equipment. We are sent out with all the equipment we can possibly use, and as we go, we make disciples.

I think the best way of translating this is "As you go, make disciples." This presents making disciples as a kind of side effect, and that is really important to understand in relation to making disciples. In life, some things that can be pulled cannot be pushed, and some things that can be pushed cannot be pulled. Making disciples is a matter of pulling people, of drawing them in through who we are and what we say.

Disciples are those who have been so ravished with Christ that others want to be like them. Others look at those disciples' life in the kingdom of God, and they say, "This is the best thing I ever saw in my life. I must have that." The best place to make disciples in the United States is in church, because there are always people there who are hungering for discipleship. They are really looking for it.

Many, many of the people who are identified as Christians have never been invited to become a disciple of Jesus. We don't have discipleship evangelism, but we need to have it because of the multitudes of people who are ready to go, who just need to understand and see and have the invitation to become disciples of Jesus. That's the way we have to go forward.

Until we go through discipleship, we can't bring people together in trinitarian fellowship, because a commitment to God, to Christ and to the Holy Spirit is not adequate to allow people to come together in the intimate form of relationship that is life transforming.

The church as the gathering of disciples is God's ideal way of bringing people to the fullness of Christ. Remember that Jesus said, "For where two or three come together in my name, there am I with them" (Matthew 18:20). Well, the Father is there in the midst. The Spirit is there in the midst. Where there are three or four thousand gathered in his name, he is in the midst. Sometimes that verse is quoted only when two to three people show up, but the important thing to realize is that Christ is in the midst, the Father is in the midst, the Spirit is in the midst; and they are building the church on that.

Now, if you have gone through discipleship and you are gathering disciples in the trinitarian presence, you are in a position to teach them to do everything Jesus said. Once again, it will not be by pushing, but by pulling. That is how you bring people to see the goodness and rightness of Christ's teachings and lead them to step into it.

The other way leads to legalism, which has repeatedly defeated the best intentions of the best of Christ's followers through the ages, because it simply does not deal with the life of the individual; it deals with the behavior. Over and over you have situations that can be cured by the changing of the person, but the person is not changed because he is pushed rather than pulled by the winsomeness of Christ. You might say, "Oh, you mustn't have anger with your brother." Then what are you going to do? Hit him on the head if he is angry with his brother? No, you have to show him why anger is not a good thing. You have to show him there is a better way of dealing with situations that provoke anger and hatred and create a spiral of injury and hurt.

A disciple is someone who is learning by going through the process of change. All the things that we moan about and talk on and on about, such as pornography, divorce and drugs, are things that can be dealt with effectively only by bringing change into the mind and the spirit, into the will, into the body and into the fellowship of the person. Then people come out saying, "Who needs that stuff? I've got something much better than that."

When you look at something like pornography and you realize the state of mind of the person who is hooked on it, you say, "This is a terrible condition to be in." You know that person can have a better way of thinking that will make the compulsion just drop off. It is the same way with hatred, with contempt and with all the things that cause the deepest problems in our families and in our communities and in our world. They all come out of an inside that is messed up, and Jesus comes and says, "Here is the way out."

BRINGING THE KINGDOM

What do the pastors and other spokespersons for Christ do? They bring the life of the kingdom to other people. They bring that life in themselves. That's what Jesus himself said, and that's what he did. When he came, he said, "Repent for the kingdom of the heavens is at hand." What was at hand? The kingdom that was in him. As people looked at him and listened to him, they realized that the kingdom of God was there and that it was available to them, and they became disciples of Jesus because of that.

Pastors and spokespersons for Christ exemplify eternal living and bring it to bear on everything around them. Eternal life is the life we have now, because our life is caught up in God's life. It is not later. What Jesus is doing is a part of what we are doing, and what we are doing is a part of what he is doing.

John 17:3 is one of the most important verses to understand: "And this is eternal life, that they may know you, the only true God, and Jesus Christ whom you have sent" (NRSV). Now, this knowing is not doctrinal knowledge; it's a living interaction with God, with his Son and with his Spirit. It is trinitarian presence in fellowship with one another that is eternal life. That is what eventually is going to come to earth. That is what has come to earth already, and we can make it a part of our lives. In so doing, we make our lives a part of God's life. So, what did Jesus preach? What was his gospel? His gospel was the availability of life in the kingdom of the heavens, or the kingdom of God, now.

Now let me ask myself something very sobering to me, and maybe to you. What is *my* gospel? What's my central message? This is the heart of our problem and of our promise. Listen to yourself when you're speaking, and ask, "What is my message?" Is my message one that pulls people into discipleship?

Now again, I don't want to be critical, but frankly, most people don't ask this question of themselves. Instead they talk about an arrangement made by God through Christ that involved his death on the cross. That is very important to understand, but ask yourself, "Is that the gospel?"

Isn't this the gospel: that when others not only hear the content of it but also see how we live it and present it, they say, "I want that. I want to be a disciple of Jesus. I want to be one of his students, learning how to live in the kingdom of God now as he lives in the kingdom of God"?

When we present the gospel through our life and our teaching of what Jesus preached, as life now available in the kingdom of God, we see people respond. I have watched it for years and have heard the testimonies of people who suddenly realize this is the gospel. This is what Jesus is about. Jesus is about bringing the life of the kingdom of God into my life now and making me a citizen of that kingdom. And then it is not over, because we spend our lives seeking the kingdom of God. As Jesus said, seek above all the kingdom of God.

Now I have to ask myself, "Do I do that, and how do I do it? Am I actually seeking the kingdom of God above all and the kind of righteousness that characterizes that kingdom?" When we do that, we can count on disciples being made. If we preach another message and live another message, we can't count on that.

That is why the work of leaders and pastors is often so hard and so full of disappointments. Their own lives are empty, and eventually they blow up. That is because they haven't heard the message that Jesus gave. They have heard another message, and perhaps with the best of intentions they were drawn into a life where they thought their job was to make things happen. But that is the worst position they can be in.

Of course, leaders need to act, but our job is not to make things happen. We live in the kingdom of God, where God is active. His Spirit is present. His Son is alive. That's where we live. If we make it happen, the result will be our converts, and we'll have to keep making them do things, because they will depend on us to jump-start them and keep them going. Instead we need to put them onto the living kingdom of God and the living Christ and allow them to live interactively, one on one, with God and to transform the world in which they live.

Discipleship is not for the church. Actually, the church is for discipleship. Discipleship is for the world, the world that God so loved, that he has great hopes for and that he is going to bring great things out of. That's where discipleship belongs. If we shrink discipleship down to church work, we will never see its power to transform ourselves or to transform the world around us. But as we step into discipleship to Christ in the great kingdom of God, out in the world as well as in the church, we begin to see a basis on which disciples can come together.

UNITY IN DISCIPLESHIP

One of the most heartbreaking things today is that we are divided between different traditions, and there is no fellowship; pastors don't care for one another because they think they are different. When we step into discipleship, we find the only basis for Christian union, the only way we can get past all the traditions and all the doctrines and all the habits and things like property that we own and who gets to control it and so on. We can come together in our communities as shepherds of Christ and deal with that world by bringing the kingdom of God through our people into the fine texture of daily living.

Discipleship isn't complicated. It is all laid out. We simply have to start with the beginning, which is Christ's authority over everything in heaven and earth, and we make disciples. We don't make Lutherans. We don't make Baptists. We don't make Catholics. We don't make Protestants. Make disciples of the Baptists, of the Lutherans, of the Catholics—of all the groups make disciples; and they will come together to form the body of Christ where they are.

Ministers can minster to one another and hold one another up and know one another without being threatened or without competing, because they are in the business of going through their community and making disciples and bringing them together and teaching them to do everything that Jesus said.

Conversation

Dallas Willard and John Ortberg

John: We have talked many times about the idea of pastors being teachers of the nations and how important that is. But when we read other folks, people who are not Christians—Richard Dawkins or Daniel Dennett or whoever— a vast majority of us know that we could not out-argue them and that we are not smarter than they are. How do we present with confidence this knowledge when we are aware that we may not be able to out-argue their position?

Dallas: One of the things that is helpful in that situation is to begin to recognize the agenda that they are working on, and it will not take you very long until you realize that a major part of their agenda is to shut you up. So they know how to work symbolisms that are provided by the institutions of knowledge in our culture that have defined the knowledge of Christ out of the domain of knowledge officially. But many times one who is not a scholar in that particular area simply has to know the history well enough to recognize that the position they are arguing is not one represented by humanity's thoughts through the ages. Only recently in this respect have we become accustomed to thinking that faith is one thing and knowledge is another.

We have people who live just around the corner from Richard Dawkins who can put him in a corner and shut him up. So it becomes a kind of contest that we have to be very careful about or we will come to despise him. The thing that he needs most to hear is the effect of love and the life of truth in human beings and then to look at what he purports to know and realize how little it has to say about what really matters for most human beings. It is the inadequacy of what is presented by knowledge in the secular world to deal with the life of the people who occupy the secular world that is the revelation of the limitations that this viewpoint, which sets the knowledge of Christ aside and says it is not knowledge, is revealed.

Now, that is something that the community has to be working on. You are right in the midst of the community up there with Stanford University, and that's an occasion where you can mix this thing up. I would hope that you would bring in some of the people who are unbelievers from Stanford, and let some others in the fellowship listen and talk, because it is only in conversation that the deficiencies are revealed. Now the conversation has been shut down, and what we need are people—writers and teachers and speakers and all kinds of people—who will simply stand up and initiate the conversation.

John: But what you are saying then is that the foundational issue isn't so much proofs for the existence for God or that sort of thing; it's the adequacy of what's being said as a foundation for life.

Dallas: That's the crucial issue, because when you've had your say one way or the other about proofs for the existence of God, which I think are extremely important, they are undermined by cheap and illogical criticisms in the minds of the students, many of whom are Christians. Then they go out and very often wind up going to seminary and having a ministry based on what, their tradition? What takes over when knowledge disappears is tradition. Jesus talked about that over and over in Matthew 15. You put the traditions of men in place of the commandments of God. Well, if the commandments of God don't constitute knowledge, why not put something else in their place? That's how it goes in human life.

John: Some might say that the name of a chapter in your book *Knowing Christ Today,* "Pastors as Teachers of the Nations," sounds presumptuous. When asked about that, your immediate response—you didn't even wait a half a second—was, "That is exactly right. Jesus is the most presumptuous person that ever lived." Say a word about what it means for all of us, if we are part of a church and trying to speak to our world today, that presumption is required.

Dallas: Well, this is an extremely important point. You know Jesus' effect on people was different from that of the scribes and Pharisees. That was because he spoke as one having authority, and people noticed that. The scribes and the Pharisees had to go look up their footnotes or find out which rabbi said this about what. The people listening to it understood that those people didn't know what they were talking about. The scribes and the Pharisees pull authority out of their connections and laid it on them, but Jesus talked about real life.

The amazing thing about Jesus—and I hope you might look carefully at the logic of his words—was how he was able to refer to reality and cause people to understand it in a different way. Usually it was in a way that got past the hardened traditions of those people who thought they were in charge of the religious life. The test of religious life is life, and that's where Jesus lived it. And that's why he refers to children and says that if you are going to enter the kingdom of God, you have to come like a little child.

Now, apart from Jesus, the next most presumptuous person in the world is a little child. They just go, you know. The main thing is, when you hear Jesus, do what he says. Don't build a theory. Just do what he says, and reality will teach you, and that is where authority ultimately lies. So, the test for the secularist and the Christian spokesperson is the reality that they bring people in touch with.

In our recent past the single greatest illustration of this is C. S. Lewis. He never pulls authority on you. He just talks about things, and he helps you see things. Multitudes of people have simply put in practice what he says, and they have found it to be true. That is the ultimate appeal of the spokesperson for Christ.

John: A question related to that one has to do with knowledge and the nature of knowledge: How would you distinguish knowledge from certainty that you are right?

Dallas: You start out with this: everyone has been certain and wrong. Certainty is a psychological state that you can work up. You see a lot of this in religious groups. They are trying to work up certainty, but that is a terrible mistake. When you convey knowledge, you are giving people things they can test and find to be true in reality.

John: What do you mean when you say "work up certainty"? Do you mean try to push themselves to feel more certainty than they really do?

Dallas: Sure. Right. I mean, this is the cheerleader. You're four hundred points behind, and there are three minutes left, so you're still saying we're going to win. If you look, you see they actually believe it. Certainty is something that is caught from the surroundings. That is true of belief, by the way. We pick up beliefs like a coat picks up lint. Little children pick up beliefs. They have to go through the process of refining that and turning that into knowledge. That should be the function of the fellowship of believers, to provide the context in which they can do that.

John: You talked about doctrine and how a lot of times we can replace being a disciple of Jesus with insisting that people have certain right doctrinal affirmations. But what is the proper role of doctrine for a disciple?

Dallas: Well, the proper role of doctrine is teaching openly with a view to people coming to understand things, not with a view to them winding up with the right views. That's not for us to control. That's for them and the Holy Spirit and reality to work out—having the right views. The problem is that doctrine is taught in a way that says you must believe this whether you believe it or not. That doesn't work well. That's why we see the steady exodus of young people from our churches. But Jesus wasn't like that. He never does that sort of thing. Anyone who can find a better way than Jesus, he would be the first to tell you to take it.

John: Would you say that one more time, because I have not heard that in churches often?

Dallas: Jesus was a man of truth. The Holy Spirit is the Spirit of truth, not of correct doctrine. I am just saying that we need to tell our young people, "Follow Jesus, and if you can find a better way than him, he would be the first to tell you to take it."

John: Isn't that dangerous?

Dallas: It's dangerous not to do that. What you wind up with is people who don't believe what they say they believe. You wind up with people—as Isaiah and then Jesus picked up—whose tongues are close to Jesus, but their hearts are far away. See, your tongue follows correctness; your heart follows truth.

John: Could you say that again?

Dallas: What gets said is an exercise in social conformity. Now sometimes that is wonderful, if it turns out that it is right, but if you think you are right, just ask someone who disagrees with you.

John: The tongue follows correctness, but the heart follows truth.

Dallas: Right. Now, that is Jesus' teaching, not mine. Check Matthew 15: "These people honor me with their lips, but their hearts are far from me" (Matthew 15:8). Now, as spokespersons for Christ, we are going for the heart. We are going for Richard Dawkins's heart. We are going for the heart of all these people, but one of the hardest things to overcome is that so many times people have not cared about that.

John: They just want to win the argument.

Dallas: That's right, absolutely right. They have this feeling that they would do anything to win the argument. What does winning the argument need? The other people to shut up. If you watch campus debates or public debates of various kinds between people like Richard and others, you see that the issue is who shuts up. That's the loser. It's like a boxing match, and that is why we as Christians, as followers of Christ, need to learn how to listen to Richard Dawkins.

John: You must be asked to debate nonbelievers sometimes. Do you do that? How do you respond to that?

Dallas: When I have been asked to do that through the years, I have always replied that I will be glad to enter a joint inquiry with so and so, but I will not debate. We will seek the truth together. That changes the situation, because the first job for someone like Richard—who is not a bad guy in many ways, but he is formed by his experience—is if you put them all in their court and say, "Now, what is the truth?" it doesn't take them five moves to begin to realize they don't get it. They are good in their specialty. That's important. Specialties are important.

At the end of the nineteenth century, specialization took over in our educational institutions. But specialization never answered the basic questions of life. Before that time, the fundamental role of education was to answer those questions. Unfortunately, the answers were often not good answers, and that put people in a position of saying, "Well, we don't even discuss this."

Often I have asked at USC and other places in public, "Has anyone shown that reality is secular? Could you show me the person and where this was done? If it has not been done, isn't it a little on the questionable side to announce we are a secular university?" Now, I know there is an administrating meaning to that, but that's not what most people pick up. They mean we don't include God in knowledge. Well, if there is a God, you might think that is a serious omission, you know. And then when you look at the disciplines and how they all are limited without a foundation, you realize this is serious intellectual work.

The tradition of Christianity has always been to lay the foundation for all of the disciplines in God, and anyone who is really interested in this issue should start with the best, with St. Thomas Aquinas—*Summa Theologica* and *Summa contra Gentiles*—and watch him do it. But you realize he was simply doing what everyone assumed had to be done. Today there is no foundation. Ultimately what rules in a discipline today is the social pressure of the best professional opinion, and that changes.

John: You say discipleship is not complicated, and yet people would say making sense of life and God is incredibly complicated. So how do you reconcile that?

Dallas: As you practice discipleship in the community of believers under the direction of—please God—pastors and spokespersons who are really living and teaching the truth that God has made available in history and Scripture and through experience, then life begins to make sense. For many of our Christians—professing Christians, perhaps serious Christians—their life doesn't make sense because they have not understood themselves. That has put them in the position where they are, and so they need teaching that will make sense of it.

That should be what comes out of our work as spokespersons for Christ. Again I reference C. S. Lewis, because most Christians are familiar with him. He makes sense of things that people never made sense of before. After reading a few of his words, they say, "Oh, I see it." Now, that light-turning-on effect should be the constant process of those of us who are followers of Christ as we go through the world and make disciples by drawing them to the truth of Christ.

John: When people say, "I believe in God, and I want to believe in God, but I have doubts sometimes; I want to follow Christ, but I fail sometimes; I am not as certain as I want to be," can they say with confidence or integrity that they know Christ? What needs to be true in their life, in their mind and their life, for them to be able to say they know Christ?

Dallas: Put his words into practice and find them to be true.

John: Is it possible that somebody might know Christ but not realize that they know Christ?

Dallas: Oh, yes. Many people know things, but they don't know that they know. That's the nature of knowledge. Like children, for example, or unsophisticates of various kinds—they don't even know what knowledge is. But our lives are filled with knowledge. You know something when you are able to deal with it as it is on an appropriate basis of thought and experience.

John: Say that one more time. You know something . . .

Dallas: You know something when you are able to deal with it as it is on an appropriate basis of thought and experience. Now, our lives are full of knowledge. Knowledge is not esoteric, and it's not rare. It is very common. It's all over the place. I like to go into university settings where you have people who have been trained to say they don't know anything and say, "Well, how does your professor grade your paper if he doesn't know anything?"

This not-knowing is a game of irresponsibility. It is a way of saying I'm not responsible. I'm an agnostic. Now, you know we never say that when something really matters. I never say that if I am in an airport and someone says what gate I am leaving from. I never say, "Well, you know, I'm an agnostic." That is true with everything that matters, because knowledge is so important. When you know something, you are able to deal with it as it is, and you are able to communicate with others about it.

And so every profession, practical and theoretical, is organized around knowledge. Imagine if electricians didn't know anything. Now, up until very recently, we didn't know anything about electricity, and that is typical of the progress of humanity under God. We come to know more and more and more. But then humanity and rebellion to God rejects knowledge of God, and that is, of course, a part of the original temptation, isn't it? Did God say . . . ? Well, but that's how it goes in life, and we should welcome opportunities to learn.

The last thing we want to do is to be arrogant and presumptuous about what we know. We want to be humble, learning. We want to ask questions and not just make assertions. As we do that, we help ourselves and other people. The most important thing we can do for young people is to help them to learn how to ask questions.

John: I would think that most of us in churches tend to think the most important thing is to give them the right answers.

Dallas: Well, we do think that, but that's the mistake. We are pushing a tradition, and we think it is very important that they get that tradition right, and if they don't, they just might go to hell. Well, of course, those are serious issues, but just getting God to inspect our minds and find that we have affirmed the right kind of thing probably isn't where we are supposed to be. That is why I said the view of salvation that is common in the message today is that you could go to heaven and have the worst sort of character imaginable, but you have had the magical moment of mental assent, and God has noted it and put it in the computer. Now, according to some groups, you have to redo it, and according to some groups you have to redo it right before you die.

John: A couple of follow-up questions on that one. One of them is, as you lay out the gospel, the simple gospel of the availability of life in the kingdom of God, it doesn't include, as you put it, the phrase "forgiveness of sins." Where does the forgiveness of sins fit in the gospel? Do you make that less central than other formulations of the gospel make it?

Dallas: I wouldn't say it is less central. It is essential, and you will not enter the kingdom of God without the forgiveness of sins. It's like the story of Abraham, see? He believed God, and it was accounted to him for righteousness. When you put your weight on Jesus and the kingdom, all of that is taken care of. One of the things that made people maddest about Jesus was his talk about how easy it is to forgive sins. Well, if I may say so, and I hope I don't mislead anyone, to forgive your sins is a load off God's mind. He is happy to do it.

John: I have never heard you say that before. Not that that makes any difference at all.

Dallas: See, this is a part of the imagery that comes in the tradition: God is mad all the time. You hear people say

God is good all the time. No, he is mad all the time.

John: God is mad all the time; all the time God is mad.

Dallas: Good mad. That is just not God. The miracle is not that God loves me; it would be a miracle if he didn't love me, because he is love. That is God's basic nature—a will to good.

John: This leads to another question that is hard to put into words. When lots of us hear you talk about how good God is, it is enormously moving, because we find there are things we think we are supposed to believe about God and then there is a way that we hope the world turns out to be. What I find myself thinking is, *He is better than what I most hoped the world could turn out to be.*

So, when you talk about things like seeking the kingdom of God, I know that is present in your mind, but for most of us, when we hear words like "seeking the kingdom of God," they have become so churchy and so superficial and so stupidly religious, we don't understand. It is the same with *disciple* and so many things. How do you break beyond the trap that I think so many of us feel? We would love to love God, but we don't know how to do that.

Dallas: Well, I need to say that is a gift, but you have to be willing to make the move. Many people are so wedded to a horrible image of God that when they read, "Seek ye first the kingdom of God," it's "straighten up or I am going to get you." We miss the whole point of the past, which is the overflowing goodness of God. We keep thinking in human terms: if God isn't mean, he can't manage the world. You can manage things only by being mean. So we have that imagery. And I think there is at least a simple answer to the question: begin to put in practice the things that Jesus said. Just begin to put them in practice—something simple like let your yes be a yes and your no be a no.

In all of Jesus' teachings, you go through a process. That's why discipleship is so important. It is a process of learning and letting your yes be a yes and your no be a no. Now, Jesus put it like this. More than that comes from what is evil. Our evangelical translators can't keep from saying "from the evil one." But it is what is evil in your heart, see? You ask yourself, *Why do I not just say it's this way or it's that way? Why do I have the endless song and dance acts that I go through to turn a yes into a no and a no into a yes?* Well, it's because of our will to manipulate people. That's the evil that it comes from. If we are willing to just let people be, to tell them how it is and how it isn't, and let that be, then we can just say, "Yes, it is this way," or "No, that's not the way it is."

John: Can I follow up on the discipleship business? If the main thing a disciple does is to try to learn from Jesus how to live and put things into practice, I think a lot of folks wrestle with this question: if you think about a Christian as "I've got the heaven issue resolved because I have affirmed the right doctrine and had the right experience," at least that feels like a really clear-cut decision. The alternative is I try to please God on my own works righteousness, and I am rejecting that and receiving forgiveness and salvation by grace through faith. So that feels clear-cut.

When Jesus was alive on earth, that seemed very clear, because he was walking around. So you were physically walking around with him or you weren't. Then in the Acts 2 church, that community was so radically different from other communities that again it felt like there was a concrete presence that helped you know, *Yup, I am a disciple because I am living with these guys that I would never be with otherwise.* In a society like ours, there are churches everywhere; it's kind of Christian, but it's kind of not Christian. If I say that a disciple is somebody who is seeking to do what Jesus says, it feels kind of fuzzy. If I do that once an hour, then do I qualify? Is it once every five minutes?

Dallas: You are seeking to learn how to do what Jesus said. You are seeking to learn how. I ask myself that question at least a few times a week. Am I a disciple today? Now, if I'm a disciple, I am learning from him. I am his student.

John: So, do you sometimes say to yourself that you are not a disciple today?

Dallas: Yes, there are occasions where I realize that I haven't learned a thing and that I haven't sought to learn a thing.

John: Is it okay if you say, "No, my eternal destiny is not in jeopardy now"?

Dallas: It is okay. God isn't breathing down your neck. Ask yourself why God did not just stay in the garden. He came around. In fact, as you read the early chapters of Genesis, God is quite chatty. Isn't that right? I mean, okay, Cain's got a problem, so I will go and talk to him. And so God gives him a little lesson and doesn't seem to help him, but God was there. I remember asking James Bryan Smith once on the platform, "Do you think God ever lets you get away with anything?" And the answer is yes, all kinds of things. That's what a life of grace is.

I'm not afraid to say that because, in a way, you've been looking for that. No, no, no—that's what you're *learning*. You are not *looking for* that. You are not looking to get away with something. But on the other hand, this is a life in which God is bringing us to the fullness of the likeness of his Son, and in order to do that, he gives us a life, and giving us a life means that we make choices and they matter; they don't have to be always correct, God isn't keeping score. That's shocking to many people, but he's not. He doesn't care about that. He cares about who we become, and he knows that as we become more like Christ, there is not going to be anything to keep score on, because he's not keeping the good things either. Normally people think he just marks down the bad things. That's a terrible view of God.

John: What does it mean then to talk about God's judgment?

Dallas: Well, he eventually has to deal with where things come out, and that will simply be a matter of declaring the truth. That will get past all of our rationalizations and explanations, and we will look at that and say, "That is true. That's what I was. That's what I did."

Now, I don't think the issue of whether you are going to heaven or hell is settled on that basis, but it's an important one. I don't mean to suggest that it's not. But I believe that the only people who will not be in heaven are people who don't want to be there. When you think about it, if you don't really like God, you don't want to be in heaven.

John: Should churches send missionaries?

Dallas: Oh, yes, absolutely.

John: Why?

Dallas: To help people to know about Christ. I mean, that's the most important knowledge on earth. We were over at Claremont Colleges in California the other night, and I looked up a foundation stone of the university system in the United States. Guess what it was? God so loved the world that he gave his only begotten Son. That was the foundation stone of the educational system of the United States from 1636, with the founding of Harvard on up into this last century. It was accepted as truth, as knowledge, as something you could inquire into and come to know if you didn't know it. What would be more important than to know that God loves the world that much?

So we need to send. People generally don't know this. They don't know this in the United States, and they need to be told. We make disciples here. I don't know how many years it took for me to understand that the Great Commission is not about foreign missions. In my ecclesiastical context, that's what it always meant.

John: Going to some other country?

Dallas: Some other country. Because, of course, we are pretty nice here.

John: One more question, Dallas. You have written a lot on Jesus' yoke being the easy yoke. When I talk with pastors, I think more and more that they just feel pressure.

Dallas: Oh, absolutely.

John: Pressure for the church to do well, pressure for them to do well. In addition, folks who aren't pastors feel pressure to be the right kind of Christian. So, could you talk a little bit about the easy yoke for pastors and for other folks in churches?

Dallas: Yes, of course. The easy yoke is to lay aside your projects and mine and to take up God's projects. I will say that again. Taking the easy yoke is to lay aside your projects or my projects, which are crushing—and this is where leaders come under intolerable pressure. It is because they are carrying their projects; they have presumed to take God's projects and made them their projects.

John: Now, when you say "lay aside my project," I assume if there's a young person with a dream of being a writer, you don't mean they shouldn't dream of being a writer—or do you?

Dallas: I mean they should not burden themselves by trying to be a writer. If they want to be a writer, they should write.

John: But not carry the outcome? Not carry the pressure?

Dallas: Absolutely right. Absolutely right. You watch someone bowling, and they turn the ball loose, and there it goes, and they stand there going, "Oomph, oomph, oomph." The thing is—I know this so well from the experience I had as a pastor for a few years, many years ago—the great temptation is to try to make it happen, whatever *it* is. That's where we need to step out of our yoke and into Jesus' yoke and let him carry the burden. But it is true with our children. It's true with writing or with whatever. We feel like we have to make it happen, and that's what we have to lay down. We don't make it happen. We turn it loose. Whatever we are doing for the Lord, we let him carry through with it.

We do our best, but we don't trust our best.

When you start trusting your best you think the solution is to work harder, and that is never the solution, especially for folks who wind up in leadership for Christ. I've rarely ever . . . I can't even remember finding someone I thought should work harder. They're working too hard. So they need to put their best into something and then leave it with God.

Of course, that's the constant teaching of the Scripture and of godly people through the ages. If you read the people who were thought of as great, whatever the tradition, you'll see they leave it with God. Mother Teresa of Calcutta is a brilliant illustration of that now—a very different way, a different spirit. And Teresa of Ávila—a wonderful person. But they learned to give it up to God.

2

WHO ARE THE EXPERTS ON LIFE TRANSFORMATION?

John Ortberg

Father, we remember now that we are right here with you and that you are in our midst and that you love us and that you long for us to be healed and whole and that we do not do any of this on our own and that this universe is a perfectly safe place for us to be and that you are closer than the air we breathe. And so we ask that you would be at work now and help us and give us energy and openness and strength, and we pray this together in Jesus' name. Amen.

JOHN ORTBERG

At the end of a class Dallas was teaching, a student was feeling arrogant and antagonistic. He raised his hand and mentioned a disagreement he had with Dallas that was both obnoxious and wrong.

A person who was at the class was waiting for Dallas to de-molish the guy, which he could easily have done. I joke some-times that I never get in an argument with Dallas, because I am afraid he will prove I don't exist. So, this student was waiting for Dallas to lower the boom. Dallas said, "Well, I think that's a good place for the class to end. Let's just stop there, and then we will pick it up next time."

Another student asked him, "Why did you do that, because you could have just let the guy have it? Why didn't you let him have it?"

Dallas's response was, "I'm practicing the discipline of not having the last word."

Every moment is a chance to be with our teacher, Jesus, and to learn how to live in the Reality. It's just that we don't see it. We think that it is just about a couple of little activities in a few small compartments of our life. Every moment is that chance. We want to learn about that together.

I first came across Dallas's work over twenty years ago when I read his book *The Spirit of the Disciplines*. I was feeling frus-trated because I wasn't changing the way that I wanted to, and in the church where I was serving, folks weren't changing the way we wanted. I got that book, and I can still remember reading the thesis statement: "Authentic transformation is possible if we are willing to do one thing and that is to arrange our lives around the kind of practices and life Jesus led to be constantly receiving power and love from the Father." The thought that transfor-mation is really possibly and that wise people have thought about it gave me so much hope. That book is now one of my prized possessions.

I ended up writing Dallas, and it turned out he lived not far from me. So I went over there, and we talked. I had the expe-rience that so many folks have with Dallas. We tell stories about him, and that's a wonderful thing, but it's really not about Dallas at all. It's about this wonder that there is a God who is as good as Jesus said that he is. Somehow, we keep losing that, and our vision of it gets distorted. But every once in a while, that vision gets cleared up, and the fog gets blown away. For whatever reason, for many of us, that has happened through the writings and the teachings of this guy, Dallas Willard.

Part of what's wonderful about him is the way he is far from perfect, as all of us are, and he has his own set of struggles. But you get the sense when you are with him that this is not just somebody who is in spiritual formation, but somebody who is actually living in the reality of the kingdom. It has taken over his body in ways that I want it to take over my body. We want to prize that and learn from it. But remember, it's not about him or about any person. It's about the reality that lies behind and can speak through any of us.

It's a lot of work—at least it is for me—just trying to keep up with him. After hearing Dallas speak, somebody said, "I feel like a whole boatload of stupid just landed on my head."

THE TROUBLE WITH LEADING THROUGH EMOTIONS

Dallas has mentioned that when he first started ministry, he thought the way that you move people is by making them feel, not by bringing them knowledge. Often leaders in the church do that. We try to create an emotional experience for people and then use that to get them to form intentions. But then, of course, the intentions fade as soon as the power of the emotions fades, and that's the nature of emotions.

What is needed is for people to actually come to see—for us to come to see—reality differently, to believe at the level of the basic ideas out of which we live, because then we don't have to hype people up into doing stuff; it flows naturally out of how things look to us.

As Dallas teaches, this is a lot of work, because it is not about trying to whip people up into a certain emotional experience. We don't want to be asking, "Was I moved by that talk?" or "How did that talk go?" but asking, "God, as we are together, would you open the windows so I can see?"

There is a charge for all of us in this to say we will work with our minds and our hearts and our wills as best we can. We'll just work. We won't sit back and listen to talks and see if that was a good talk, but we will roll up our sleeves and work. And then we will ask God, "What do you have in this for me?" and maybe "What do you have in this for us, if it is true that the church is at a decisive point?" Then there could be a movement to recapture, in our day, the beauty of the vision of God's kingdom. I don't know what that is, but we need to be asking the question "God, are you doing something right now, and could you help us know what that is?"

Who Will Teach Us?

Now the question is "Who are the experts on life transformation in our day? Who really knows what life can be and how we can pursue it?" Human beings are creatures that have to learn. Whether or not we want to, we are just that kind of a being. So we will always search for teachers, but we tend to do that particularly when we know that we don't know.

I was recently thinking about the piano teacher my sister and I had when we were little. Mrs. Beyer was German, and when I tell you she was German, you know everything about her you need to know. She would tell us how short to clip our fingernails and what our posture should be. She even told our parents that the piano we had at our house was not adequate, so they needed to go and buy a new piano. And they did. When my sister and I finally wanted to quit taking lessons, we were all afraid to tell

Mrs. Beyer. My dad offered me five dollars to call Mrs. Beyer and tell her. So I did.

We humans are the kind of beings that have to be taught, whether it's to play the piano or to play tennis or to live. We learn first from our parents and then from other folks around us—our coworkers and our boss and our culture. The difficulty is that—especially in our day, when we have decided that authority is suspect—we don't think of ourselves as having to learn how to live. And so we never ask ourselves the question "Who has mastered life? Who is worthy of being the teacher that I sit under?"

Many people think of Jesus as our Savior, as the one who will get us into heaven. So the question often is "Have I accepted Jesus as my Savior?" But we never ask the question "Have I accepted Jesus as my teacher?" And that's the real question. With the disciples, it began there. They began by accepting him as their teacher, and then accepting him as their Savior—which included, of course, their eternal destiny—was a natural outflow of that. But they started with Jesus as their teacher, because we all have to learn how to live.

Two Approaches to Wisdom

Psalm 1 is a classic expression of where we find wisdom. We are all looking for wisdom about how to live, and Israel cherished this Scripture because they loved wisdom so much.

> Blessed are the people who do not walk in the counsel of the ungodly or stand in the way of sinners or sit in the seat of mockers, but their delight is in the law of the Lord, and on that law, they meditate day and night. Such people are like trees planted by streams of water which yield fruit in season and whose leaves do not wither. Whatever they do prospers. Not so with the wicked. They are like the chaff that the wind

blows away; therefore, the wicked will not stand in the
judgment nor sinners in the assembly of the righteous, for
the Lord watches over the way of the righteous, but the way
of the wicked shall perish. (Psalm 1 paraphrased)

This psalm is an expression of two ways of approaching wisdom.
We all live by default or by design, and the psalmist is saying that
we live in a world where just to drift is disaster. He talks about
this by using the old language: blessed is the person who does
not live, or walk, in the counsel of the ungodly.

Now, what is the counsel of the ungodly? I grew up in a Baptist
church, so I would think the counsel of the ungodly is somebody
encouraging me to go smoke a cigarette or have sex or be an
atheist or something like that. Dallas says that the counsel of the
ungodly is just the way most people talk. It is the counsel to live
as though it were not true that you are an unceasing spiritual
being with an eternal destiny in God's glorious universe. The
counsel of the ungodly is "Live as if it matters what people think
of you." The counsel of the ungodly is "Live as if the outcomes
of your life are on your shoulders and you control them." The
counsel of the ungodly is "Live as if aging is something to worry
about." The counsel of the ungodly is "Live as if satisfying your
desires and appetites is central to your well-being and a wise
strategy for living." That's the counsel of the ungodly. It goes on
all the time, and we rarely even see it.

I pulled into a gas station not too long ago, and there was this
sign that said, "We help you move faster." Now, is that the main
need I have? That would be the counsel of the ungodly.

Here's another example: One day when our daughter was
little, I was helping her ride her bike, and I had a Band-Aid on
my arm. She asked what it was there for, and I explained that I
had just been given an examination because I had taken out life

insurance. I am kind of a feeler, so I thought this would be a chance to get, you know, tender feelings from my daughter. I said I had that done because I love my family so much and I want to make sure that if anything happens to Daddy, the family is taken care of. So, I said, "Because of this, the arrangement is, if I die, you get two hundred thousand dollars."

Her eyes got big and she said, "Apiece?"

We hear the counsel of the ungodly as soon as we arrive in this world, and all we have to do is turn on a television, go online, or listen to conversations through the day to know that what they encourage is acquiring more, being more successful, looking younger and sexier, and getting even with those who hurt you. Just listen to the conversations we have with each other, and that's the counsel of the ungodly.

It's very interesting how there is a progression in Psalm 1. First it says, "Blessed is the man who does not walk in the counsel of the wicked," and then the next step is "or stand in the way of sinners."

The idea here is that it's not just your thinking that's been influenced. You find your way of life affected. You begin to conform. First you are walking with folks, and then you are standing with them. The next phase beyond that is sitting "in the seat of the mockers." Now, when I sit down, I'm not going anywhere. I've just decided this is where I am going to stay. And that's what can happen in a life. You walk in that way and then you stand there and then you sit down there. Nobody plans to do that. Nobody plans to go on a destructive way. It just happens. It's the drift of the world. So, that's one way.

Then the psalmist says there is another way, and that is the way of a person who doesn't do that, but rather who delights in the law and the way and the plan for life and the power and the presence of God. That's the life that can flourish. That's the life that can be good. So, there's a decision that everybody faces, and part of the danger of the world is it causes us to forget that we have to decide who we are going to learn to live from. We don't even view that as a live question, but everybody decides, and each of us goes one way or another.

JESUS AND THE WORLD

Human beings cannot help looking for someone to teach us how to live. This is why it is so important for those of us who want to follow Jesus and for those of us who help to lead churches to know that Jesus is the best and only one from which human beings should learn how to live. Just Jesus.

We all learn somewhere. We learn first from our parents and then our coworkers or bosses, the media, the culture and people around us. The Bible says all attempts to do things that don't start with God will betray us.

Dallas speaks about how we are to deal with voices that point away from Jesus; the ultimate issue is their inadequacy to provide a foundation for life to the people who follow them. They can't provide a foundation. They can't teach us how to live. You see the apostle Paul talking about this: "For Christ did not send me to baptize, but to preach the gospel—not with words of human wisdom, lest the cross of Christ be emptied of its power. For the message of the cross is foolishness to those who are perishing, but to us who are being saved it is the power of God." Then he goes on: "Where is the wise man? Where is the scholar? Where is the philosopher of this age? Has not God made foolish the wisdom of the world?" (1 Corinthians 1:17-18, 20).

This doesn't mean it's not good to learn and to think deeply. Of course it does not mean that. It means that the way the world truly operates—by the wisdom of God, which is dying in order to live and being last in order to be first, the law of inversion—

will always look like folly in our world. Other voices are promoted and get heard, but they ultimately lead to death.

PSYCHOLOGY AND THE CHURCH

In our day, psychology has been an attempt to find a way to give wisdom to human beings about how to live. Because it's an attempt to apply science, we assume that only science has knowledge regarding how we should live. One of the reasons psychology has become so popular is because often the church has not done this well.

Richard Lovelace has written an interesting book on spiritual formation called *Renewal as a Way of Life*. He talks in it about sin and the nature of sin, and that historically the church has understood the human condition as very, very complex, and there was good language for all that. Then, around the end of the nineteenth century, a very simplistic, superficial kind of Victorian morality began to predominate. It became very black or white: divorced people are bad, married people are good, and so on.

Then along came Freud, and he talked about tremendous complexity and about levels and layers of human existence. It was called depth psychology because it was so deep. People looked at it and said, "Yes, that describes my experience of myself. That gives me language, because I find that I am such a complex being." The church at its best had always understood that, but when that gets lost, when it just becomes superficial moralizing, people look someplace else to help give them the language to describe the complexity and the depth of human existence. So, in our day, psychology tends to be the place where folks look for that. And the vast majority of folks in influential seats in the discipline of mental health are much less likely to believe in God, to follow God, than the population in general.

Over the last twenty years or so, probably the biggest

movement in psychology has been the development of what is sometimes called positive psychology. Psychology has tended to put most of its efforts south of the equator in human pathology. How do you deal with manic depressive disorder or associative disorders or severe anxiety? That's probably because this is where psychology has tended to be most successful, partly because medication can often help.

BEING GOOD AND HAVING A GOOD LIFE

There's been an increasing hunger to know how we help people to flourish, not just get rid of pathology. And once you get into how you help people flourish, you're right back to Psalm 1. What does a flourishing life look like? So ethics have to become a part of psychology. Questions of meaning have to become a part of psychology. And it's very difficult to find a secular foundation for that.

Folks who write in this area tend to look back at history, because science doesn't do a very good job of asking some basic questions: What is a good life? What is a good person? They tend to quote Aristotle, the classic or stoic traditions, Confucius or Buddha. Guess who they have a hard time quoting? Jesus—even though we live in a culture that has been shaped in its understanding of good by Jesus and the movement around him far, far, far more than by anybody else.

But we live in a world where, for a whole variety of reasons (some of which are the church's fault), that is become increasing inaccessible. If you are part of a church, if you help to lead a church, you are a steward of this gospel, of this way of Jesus. Jesus has the best knowledge—the best information—about how to live. Jesus still has the best knowledge and the best information about what a good person is and how you become one. We cannot get away from our need for that.

Dallas talks about four questions that everybody has to wrestle with. One is "What's reality?" Another one is "What's the good life?" We can't stop wondering about that. Another one is "Who is a good person?" The fourth is "How do you become a good person?" We cannot stop wrestling with these questions.

It is very interesting that those who have the good life tend to be the focus of advertisements: people with thick hair and white teeth and fresh breath and big houses and new cars. That's the good life. But what's a good person? Just listen to people's complaints and all kinds of language about the moral character of those they work with. It's often impolite language, so I won't repeat any of the words, but we can't get away from evaluating whether others are good or not. At a person's funeral, we talk about whether or not he or she was a good person. That is why obituaries are very different from advertisements. Dallas will say that you very rarely read an obituary describing someone as having a full head of hair and white teeth and a nice car.

When we get to the end our life, we hope people will say we were good, but we live our lives asking how we can get the good life. We have lost the sense that there is a connection between being a good person and living a good life. Jesus understood that only the person who is becoming good, as God views and intends good, is able to live the good life. Our hunger for both will never go away. Jesus has the best knowledge about this, and you and I are stewards of that—and the world needs it desperately.

What Is the Gospel?

If you had to answer the question "What is the gospel that Jesus himself preached?" how would you respond? I grew up in the church, so I sure believed that I understood the gospel, but when Dallas posed the question in that way, I didn't know the answer. From the beginning, the Gospel of Mark, we learn that after John the Baptist was put in prison, Jesus went into Galilee, proclaiming the good news of God. Now, the good news, *euangelion*—that's the gospel. As Jesus went into Galilee proclaiming the good news of God, he said, "The time has come. The kingdom of God is near. Repent and believe the good news"—believe the gospel, the *euangelion* (Mark 1:14-15).

In all three of the Synoptic Gospels, Matthew, Mark and Luke, a nearly identical summary is given of the basic gospel that Jesus proclaimed at the very beginning of his ministry. He chose his twelve disciples, and he began to get on with his ministry. We are told, "After this, Jesus traveled about from one town and village to another, proclaiming the good news of the kingdom of God" (Luke 8:1).

In the next chapter, Jesus sends out the twelve disciples, telling them to go out and preach the kingdom of God. Then he sends out the seventy-two, and he tells them to go out and heal the sick and proclaim the kingdom of God. This is the whole ministry.

Then Jesus is crucified. He is resurrected. And then "he appeared to [his disciples] over a period of forty days and spoke about the kingdom of God" (Acts 1:3). In the very last verse in the book of Acts, the apostle Paul is in Rome in chains, and "boldly and without hindrance he preached the kingdom of God" (Acts 28:31).

If you had to summarize in a single phrase the gospel that Jesus preached, it would be "the kingdom of God." The kingdom of God has always existed. That was not new with Jesus. What was new with Jesus was that the kingdom of God had become available for human beings to enter into and live in. That's his gospel: the kingdom of God is now available, and if you want to, you can come right on in and live in it. It is tragic that the gospel of Jesus has been substituted for another cheaper, powerless gospel—what might be called the gospel of minimal entrance requirements for getting into heaven when you die.

The picture I use for this is from *Monty Python and the Holy Grail*. At the end of that film, Arthur and his little band are trying to get across a giant chasm, because the castle—the good place—is on the other side. The quest is to get to the other side, but there is a bridge keeper, and he asks them each three questions they have to answer correctly in order to get across. If they get the answers wrong, they will be cast down into an abyss.

He asks the first knight, "State your name," and he does. Then, "State your quest," and he does. Then the bridgekeeper asks, "What is your favorite color?" The knight says red, and he's amazed that he is able to get across the bridge so easily.

The second knight comes up, and he is quite confident. The bridge keeper asks him the first two questions, and he answers those correctly. Then he asks who won the World Cup in 1948, or something like that. The knight says, "I have no idea," and he is cast down into the abyss.

So the third knight is terrified. But he also answers the first two questions correctly. Then he is asked, "What's your favorite color?" He is so nervous, he says, "Red—no, blue!" He's thrown into the abyss.

Arthur is the last one, and the bridge keeper asks him to state his name. "I'm Arthur, king of the Britons."

"What's your quest?"

"The Holy Grail."

"What's the air speed velocity of an unladen swallow?"

"Well, that depends. An African swallow or European swallow?"

The bridge keeper says, "I don't know that," and he is cast into the abyss.

A lot of people's idea of the gospel is that the big question is "How do you know you're going to get into heaven when you die?" which ends up meaning, "Have you satisfied the minimal entrance requirements?" The gospel becomes the announcement of the minimal entrance requirements for getting into heaven when you die. Here is the problem: Where in the New Testament does Jesus ever say, "Now I will tell you the minimal entrance requirements for getting into heaven when you die"? Nowhere.

The gospel is never presented that way, because it can't be by its nature. If my goal is to get into heaven when I die, I have a cartoonish view of heaven as a pleasure factory and hell as a torture chamber. I think that I want to get into heaven when I actually don't want God at all. This is hopelessly distorted by wrong thinking about God and heaven and the afterlife and the good life and a good person. God uses it sometimes as a beginning point for people, because God is a gracious God, but it is utterly unconnected with the call to be a disciple of Jesus.

Our Kingdoms and the Kingdom of God

Jesus' gospel is not this: "How do you know you're going to get into heaven when you die? In case you are not clued in on that, here are the minimum entrance requirements." His gospel is "Now the kingdom of God is available." Jesus says that life is the presence and power of God come to earth in him, in his body. Heaven is on earth, literally. Jesus says, "Look at it, and if you want it, just come and be with me and watch me and learn from me and try to do what I do."

Let's talk for a few moments about the kingdom. This gospel of Jesus, of course, includes the free promise of the forgiveness of sins by grace alone. It includes the promise that death is not going to be the end. It includes all of that. There's a corporate dimension to it, but it speaks to individuals very, very deeply as well. But it is more than the forgiveness of sins, and it is more than just what will happen to me after I die.

A lot of people think the only real reason Jesus came was to die on the cross. That is not the only reason. Jesus came as the kingdom bringer. His gospel was the availability of the kingdom. His purpose was to manifest the kingdom. His one command was to pursue the kingdom: "Seek ye first the kingdom of God." His one plan was to extend the kingdom. But many people do not understand the phrase *the kingdom of God*, because it's in archaic language. We don't use that kind of language much. We don't have kings in this country. Kingdoms are kind of odd.

A kingdom, Dallas would say, is the range of your effective will; that is, your kingdom is the little sphere in which things happen just because you want them to happen. This is the real core of what it means to be made in the image of God. God says, "Let us make humankind in our image, according to our likeness; and let them have dominion" (Genesis 1:26 NRSV). *Dominion* is kingdom language. To exercise dominion means to find out that my will is actually effective, actually makes a difference, actually can make things happen.

After a child is born, he begins to learn that he has a kingdom. What's a two-year-old's favorite word? *No.* What's his next favorite word? *Mine.* Why? He's learning that he has a kingdom. *No* is a really important kingdom word. *Mine* is a really important kingdom word. Children get into the backseat of the car, and what do they do? They draw a little line and they say, "You can't come over that line." So they are learning about kingdoms. "You stay in your kingdom." And then they violate each other's kingdoms. Then Dad gets upset with this and sends Mr. Hand like a snake back to the back seat, because whose kingdom does Dad think the car is? He thinks it is his kingdom, so they all retreat to get away from Mr. Hand. Kent Davis says a little tap on the brakes brings them right into play. Thy kingdom come, you know.

We all have kingdoms, and understanding this is basic to understanding human nature and human dignity. This is one reason leadership is so hard. It's very difficult to lead people without violating their kingdoms. That's why we are sensitive when we are manipulated or flattered or intimidated: somebody is violating our kingdom. Of course, we do this in churches all the time. But as Dallas teaches and interacts, he works hard at not violating kingdoms, because kingdom violation is kind of like a spiritual steroid. You can build a church that way, but it's not going to last, because God has given each person a will. Everybody has a little lock on the door of their heart, and nobody, not even God himself, can force that open.

We all have kingdoms, and the basic problem of the human condition is that our kingdoms have been junked up by sin. This is just one of the things that the world apart from God doesn't understand. Our kingdoms are wrong, and that wrongness is in our body, in our will, and in our mind; it's much, much, much deeper than we are aware of.

There is a little cartoon I saw not too long ago trying to pose a solution for our world. The idea is that education will save the human race. But education, at least as is commonly understood as more information, will not save the human race. At a conference years ago, Dallas put a sign up on the wall that said, "The will is transformed by experience, not information." Both inside the church and out, we tremendously overestimate the power of information to bring about transformation.

All of our kingdoms intersect with others' kingdoms. We get married. We have families. We live in neighborhoods. We go to schools. We have corporations. We have nations. All of those kingdoms merge and connect and interweave and mesh with each other, and we might call that whole conglomeration of all those systems and all those kingdoms "the kingdom of the earth."

JESUS INTRODUCES US TO THE KINGDOM

How are things going in the kingdom of earth? Not so well. Then Jesus comes, and he says that there is another kingdom, and it's real—more real by far than you can understand. The reality of this kingdom is what wise people stake their existence on. Jesus calls it the kingdom of God.

A lot of what Jesus does when he teaches is try to correct people's distorted ideas about the kingdom of God. Again, when I listen to Dallas teach, I realize that the kingdom is what I want more than anything else. That's what would happen with Jesus. That is why he would so often say, "You have heard it said, but I say to you . . ."

And he would tell stories: "What shall I compare the kingdom of God to? It's like a guy who finds a treasure in a field." Now, why does Jesus tell that story? Because when somebody finds a treasure, they want it. They want it *really* bad. Jesus is saying that when something passes the litmus test and you know you'll honor it, you'll want it more than you have ever wanted anything in your life.

"YOUR KINGDOM COME"

The right vision of the kingdom isn't just theologically accurate. It will awaken tremendous desire in you. It will awaken; it can't be forced and it can't be manipulated. It simply has to be a vision of what is true that evokes a desire in us that is stronger than our desire for anything else, because we know that to have it would be better than to have anything else.

Paul understands this. He says that the kingdom of God is not about rules over eating or drinking (Romans 14:17). We always do that to the kingdom. We distort it. We legalize it. Then it becomes exhausting and undesirable. The kingdom of God is not about rules over eating or drinking; it is about righteousness, peace and joy. That's the kingdom of God. It's about doing real well.

There's the kingdom of God and there's the kingdom of earth, and Jesus' plan is to bring up there down here. I don't know why I did not see this for so long. I'm in a church where we say the Lord's Prayer all the time—"Your kingdom come"—but I did not know what it meant.

I lived in Chicago in the 1980s, back when the Chicago Bears were coached by Mike Ditka, and William "Refrigerator" Perry was a defensive lineman. At a Bears chapel service, Perry was asked to pray the Lord's Prayer, and Ditka leaned over to the chaplain and said, "I'll bet you twenty bucks the Fridge does not know the Lord's Prayer."

The chaplain thought it was kind of weird to be betting on the Lord's Prayer, but said, "Okay, I will take you up on it."

They all bowed their heads, and the Fridge started to pray: "Now I lay me down to sleep, I pray the Lord . . ." Ditka just shook his head, handed over the twenty dollars, and said, "I was sure he didn't know the Lord's Prayer."

"Our Father, who art in heaven . . . " Heaven is not someplace way out there, far away; it's the range of God's effective will. It can be right here, closer than the air we breathe. That's good news. "Our Father, who art in heaven, hallowed be thy name." May people come to see how wonderful and good you are. "Your kingdom come, your will be done, on earth as it is in heaven." Now the question is, do you believe that can happen?

When anyone got in trouble on *Star Trek*, they would pray a little prayer to Scotty: "Beam me up." I used to think that was what the church prayed: "The world is going to hell. It's a bad place. Beam me up. Get me out of here so I can get from down here to up there." When Jesus gives us the prayer to pray, he does not tell us to say, "God, beam me up. Get me out of here so

I can go from down here to up there." Instead he says to pray, "Make up there come down here."

"Your kingdom come." Where? Well, first in my body. How does that happen? What does that look like? And from there it comes into my relationships, into our churches, into this world. "Your kingdom come. Your will be done, on earth as it is in heaven." That's what we are stewards of. That's the best information on life transformation ever given to the human race.

Question and Answer

with John Ortberg

Question: Dallas makes the point about not worrying about teaching correct doctrine, but basically to teach what Jesus taught and to live into that. So how would you explain to someone the difference between teaching doctrine and what Dallas is talking about?

John: It's a great question. One of the challenges, particularly with Dallas, is he uses words in such a precise way and often such a loaded way that it takes a while to unpack them, or there will be an assumption that we are tracking and know how the word is being used.

Here's what I would say is the issue he is trying to address. Often in churches, we try to get people to affirm the right beliefs, the right points of view. The real test of what I actually believe is "Does it guide what I do?" For example, if I am up on a skyscraper, I would never step off, because I believe in gravity. I don't have to force myself to believe in gravity. I don't have to hype myself. I just believe in gravity. So I won't step off that roof unless I am trying to hurt myself.

My actions are always a result of my intentions and my perceptions of how things are. Sometimes in churches we work to get people to affirm stuff, even though they don't believe in it like they believe in gravity. So somebody will say, "I believe that the Bible is the inspired, authoritative Word of God." But the Bible says it is more blessed to give than to receive, yet they are not giving.

So, do they really believe that the Bible is the authoritative, inspired Word of God? Well, at one level, they think they do, but the most important level of belief is their mental map of reality. What are those perceptions that actually guide how we live, what we do? Because that is simply how reality looks to us. What we want to do is not simply teach doctrine and get people to affirm it. We want to help people have the same mental map that Jesus had of how things are.

For example, one time somebody in church came up and asked me, "What do we believe about the Trinity?" If I just say what we believe, and they say okay, they are not actually believing something. They're just giving affirmation to it. Now, Dallas would say the point of believing in the Trinity is not that you get an A from God in theology. What's the value of believing that two plus two equals four? Well, you will know how many apples are in the house. You will be able to deal with reality better. That is part of what we talked about. A true belief enables you to deal with reality. That's what we want to do: we want to teach Jesus and his teachings so that people come to believe it with their whole selves, so that they are able to navigate the reality of God and life and other people and temptation well.

So, doctrine properly understood is tremendously important, but if we think about doctrine as a separate, abstract series of statements that people need to affirm to get an A on their theology exam, but they become divorced from how it applies to actual living, it does no good at all. If I say that I believe that God is love, and I get that right on a theology test, when I am actually a jerk in my relationships with other people, then I have not come to the kind of belief that Jesus is interested in.

Question: As we are teaching Christian formation, every once in a while, I run into a person who is so welded to their performance-driven approach and the try-harder Christianity that when we try to explain that it's based on a relationship with God, they think we are teaching license. I wonder if you have run into that and if you have developed a good way of cracking that shell.

John: I don't know of a good, short answer for that question. Dallas says that spiritual transformation is different from behavior modification. The point isn't that isolated behaviors like cheating or lying are unimportant, because they are very important. The point is that, if the inner stream of people's thoughts and feelings don't get changed, they will never get good enough at suppressing behavior to be transformed people. The aim—I think Dallas said that this is a key point of controversy between Jesus and the Pharisees—the Pharisees' aim in the New Testament, as most of those conflicts are described, was to get people to do right things. But Jesus' aim was for people to become the sort of persons who would automatically do right things.

That's a hugely different aim, because I can do the right thing in the moment, but it can go against the grain of everything I want to do inside, and the goal is to transform the person inside so that doing the right thing is the natural outcome of that. That's as far away from license as can be. It's actually infinitely more challenging to be changed from the inside than it is to do behavior modification. But it's also recognizing that if we just go after behavior modification and say, "Try harder; grit your teeth more to do it," it will never bring about the deeper level of transformation that's the only hope for a human being. It's actually, in many ways, the opposite of license. It's just aiming at the root instead of at the symptoms.

Question: You and Dallas alluded to the will being transformed by experience and not information. Can you speak to the difference between information and knowledge?

John: I will give it my best shot. I think knowledge is probably, as Dallas would say, "When I believe something to be true and it is true." Knowledge would be when I believe something is true, and I believe it for good reasons; it wasn't just a lucky guess, and in fact, it is true. So it would be something inside a person. Information would simply be a description, like a statement on a piece of paper. It becomes knowledge when I come to believe it and it's true. So information could be outside a person, but it becomes knowledge when we absorb it and it becomes true.

Question: Could you speak to what it does to the soul when we are asked to believe something we actually don't believe or we're asked to espouse something we actually don't? So, when we are passing on that doctrine, but somebody doesn't actually believe it, yet in an evangelical church they are actually told to proclaim it, what does that do to the soul?

John: The soul is the deepest part of us that integrates our will and our mind and our bodies. The soul cries out for the person to be integrated, to be whole. Any time that doesn't happen, the soul gets damaged. If a person tries to produce a sense of certainty by willpower, they actually have to damage their mind.

For me, it is helpful to make distinctions among faith, certainty and commitment. It is very helpful to distinguish those. Certainty is a feeling that I cannot generate by willpower. I'm a Cubs fan; how certain am I that the Cubs will win the pennant this year? Well, I'm not very certain, and it would not be wise for me to try to conjure up a deeper level of certainty. Certainty is a byproduct of knowing, and so what I can do is seek to know more, but if I try to generate a feeling of certainty by willpower, I damage my mind, because my mind knows that certainty is not appropriately generated by willpower. It's a byproduct of studying and knowing. That's why we should never ever try to get people to feel pressured or forced to generate a feeling of certainty. Never.

Now, commitment is a different thing. I can commit myself to a person, to a marriage, to my children, to a cause, even though I have various levels of certainty about that person or about what the outcome will be. In my relationship with Jesus, I always can commit myself to him. I can seek to do what he would tell me to do. I cannot cause myself to have a different level of certainty than what I actually have. At least not directly.

Question: Dallas has been a mentor to me through his books and through the Internet, but it seems, as is in the Gospels, Jesus is personal and intentional with spending time with people. With Dallas mentoring and you discipling others, how is it that you practically go about discipling somebody? I think sometimes we assume that it is curriculum and teaching these things, but what are some practical things that Dallas did to disciple you, and how do you disciple others? How do we actually go about that, as opposed to just giving information and doctrine?

John: For me with Dallas, it has mostly been being exposed to the kind of person that he is. The first time I talked with him, I went over to his house. I was the pastor of a little church, a very young pastor, and when I sat down and started to talk with him, the phone would ring—this was back before there were answering machines—and he wouldn't answer the phone. He would just talk with me like he had nothing more important to do. When I was with him, hurry was not in his body. Somebody said of Dallas one time, "I would like to live in his time zone."

Mostly I would watch how he lived, and I would think, *I want to live that way.* Now, certainly there would be times when he would recommend something to read, and that can be a helpful thing. And there will be moments of crisis. I remember one time when I hit the most painful moment in my life so far, and I had told a few people that I know really well about it, and it was really raw. The response I would get from folks was generally sympathy and support, which I appreciated. I told Dallas, and there was a long pause—with Dallas, there's always a long pause—then he said it would be a test of my joyful confidence in God. I don't know of anybody else that sentence would have come out of, but it was exactly right. It was just what I needed to hear. So, when there is an important spiritually formative relationship, in moments of crisis, they have contact and are able to talk together— that's a really important thing.

The one other thing I will say about that is we sometimes use *disciple* differently. In churches, we talk about this person discipling somebody else. The New Testament never talks about one person discipling another person. In the New Testament we are all disciples of Jesus. Discipling isn't the kind of thing that one person or one program or one curriculum can do, because it has to do with learning how to do life. We are actually in the process of learning how to do life, of being shaped, all the time.

I think if we talk about discipling with the wrong kind of language, it makes it sound like a very narrow relationship with a very narrow set of interactions and programs, and like it can actually take care of the soul or the spiritual life. It is important to understand that, no, being a disciple is a full-time job, and it will require me thinking about my life 24/7. But there will be certain people in my life that really help me understand Jesus or help me move toward that, and so I want to lean into those folks a lot.

The last thing I will say about this one is that Gary is working with the Dallas Willard Center for Christian Spiritual Formation to help churches get really practical and wise and deep around what discipleship looks like.

Question: I was looking at what transformed people look like—1 Corinthians 13 and 2 Peter 1:1-11. What I am wondering is the correlation between that and spiritual discipline. I want that.

John: The danger is always that we think of a transformed person in terms of devotional practices, but those are a means to an end. The goal, the end, to which they are a means is love. That is why 1 Corinthians 13 is in there. So a transformed person is somebody who genuinely loves God and genuinely loves other people.

Then the question is, what are the means by which I can pursue transformation toward becoming loving and joyful? Always the danger in churches is measuring how often somebody goes to church, how much they read the Bible, how much they are part of a small group. We measure people's spiritual maturity in terms of their devotional practices. The problem with that is, back in Jesus' day, if you measured people's spiritual maturity in terms of their devotional practices, who would come out on top? The Pharisees. We have to measure spiritual maturity in such a way that the Pharisees don't win. Otherwise, we'll just produce Pharisees. But in churches, that's what we do a lot, because we try to mass produce it and put everybody through a program. We measure devotional practices instead of what kind of persons we are actually producing.

3

How to Step into the Kingdom and Live There

Dallas Willard

Lord, you will have to be our teacher, because the dignity has been drained out of us in so many ways. We have been treated like dirt, and that has stuck on us. We've put ourselves against standards of our own making, because we thought it would give us worth. Please touch each person with how unique they are in your eyes and how their dignity in your eyes is so great that you will not even override them; you will woo them and pursue them and help them to accept that you are seeking them and you will allow yourself to be found by them if they simply cry out for help. I pray that great freedom will come across them because of their awareness of where they stand in your kingdom. That will make Jesus very happy, and the angels in heaven will jump up and down. And so we say, Let it be so, and that's what we mean by amen. Amen.

Dallas Willard

*J*esus' invitation to the easy yoke is based on his dignity and on the knowledge he brings and what he gives to us. We must understand that what we bring is absolutely essential, unique; it isn't provided by anyone else.

I am old enough to know all the old hymns, and I still love to sing,

> Rescue the perishing, care for the dying,
> Snatch them in pity from sin and the grave;
> Weep o'er the erring one, lift up the fallen,
> Tell them of Jesus, the mighty to save.

As Jesus looked out at the crowds of people, he said his heart was torn within him, because they were like sheep scattered abroad, having no shepherd. That is exactly where we stand today.

Part of what has been happening to the church and its response to the needs of the current age is that ministry has begun to spread out, and we are beginning to understand that ministry is for everyone who is a follower of Christ, wherever they may be. To live in the kingdom of God and to bring the message of the kingdom of God to the people who are there in a loving, attractive, forceful way is the gift that comes to every person who is a follower of Jesus Christ.

The way you live in the easy yoke is by following the Great Commission. Church *works* with the Great Commission. You begin with discipleship, and you bring disciples together in trinitarian fellowship, and it is the Trinity that is doing the work, and you get to watch. With that foundation, it is easy to lead people into obedience, but if you don't have that foundation, it is simply impossible. You'll wind up with people who are following traditions of men, following legalistic dictates of some kind—on themselves, perhaps more mercilessly than on anyone else.

And goodbye to the easy yoke. At that point, you are going to have a hard yoke, and you will have to pull the load by yourself, but when we step into the message of Jesus of the kingdom of God, we step into that. We become bearers of the kingdom, and a part of that is to explain and proclaim.

Jesus did three things in his own ministry: proclaim the availability of the kingdom of God to everyone, regardless of their standing in life; teach what it was like; and manifest its presence in events that could not be explained in a natural way. He is the master of that, and he invites us to step into that and to watch it happen where we are. It may be in a large church. It may be in a small church. It may be in an office. It may be in the responsibilities of a politically elected official.

Through the ages, it has always been true that when Christ was living vitally in his people, even if they lived in a desert, the people who had the responsibilities of government realized they had to have help from them. So there was a steady path of government officials out into the desert to talk to St. Anthony as he was weaving his mats and being silent and fighting with Satan.

The truth of the matter is, there is no solution apart from what we have to bring. Hold your head high in the dignity of what you have to give and what has been given to you. There is no other source, and when we take a verse like "there is no other name under heaven given to men by which we must be saved" (Acts 4:12) and look at it and think only in terms of making it into the cool place, we drain the verse of its significance.

Salvation is deliverance—manifold kinds of deliverance. That is what enables us to stand in life and let the water of life flow through us to everyone around us, and then we just observe the results. We don't make it happen. The burden is not ours. The

Lord will take care of it, and we have to get out of his way and stop messing with things that we should leave to his care. Then we will see the result, and we will know the reality of the easy yoke. And we will live with joy and power where we are, for now and for the future.

The topic I want to stress is how to step into the kingdom and live there. It's one thing to hear the message. It's one thing to be told the kingdom is right here. By the way, when you read the translations, do understand that the message is not that the kingdom is near but not yet here, or that it's about to come but it hasn't come yet. The message is that it has come to you. It is now available to anyone who will identify through the presence of Christ and become his disciple. But the real issue is, how do you do that?

THE KINGDOM IS HERE; SEEK IT

Now, when we think about how to do this, we have to pay attention to the fact that stepping into the kingdom is a gift. It's God's part and our part. God is faithful to take care of his part. It is much like gravity. You couldn't walk without gravity, but if you wait on gravity to make you walk, you will never walk. It's there. It's in process, and God is seeking those who would worship him in spirit and in truth. God is not indifferently sitting back, waiting. He is active. He is in the world, and seeking is the key to understanding how to enter into the kingdom of God and live there.

One of the problems that many Christians today have is that, since they are Christians, they have found it and they stop seeking. But seeking is the way we live. We never get beyond seeking, and it has many dimensions. One of the most important is that God wants to be wanted. He wants to be sought. That is why he doesn't just run over us. He is there with the new birth from above.

You may not have noticed that in John 3 the discussion is about how to see and enter the kingdom of God. It's now. Nicodemus is having some problems with it. He doesn't really understand it, though he is a teacher in Israel, and he comes to Jesus, talking as if he did understand. Jesus helped him see he did not understand and helped him to understand what it is like to live in the kingdom of God.

GRACE, AND SOME SHOCKING WORDS

The great teachings of grace are fundamental in understanding how to step into the kingdom and live there. It's by grace that we are brought to life, as Ephesians 2 tells us. While we were dead in trespasses and sin, God quickened us. I love this verse from a wonderful old Wesleyan hymn:

> Long my imprisoned spirit lay,
> Fast bound in sin and nature's night;
> Thine eye diffused a quickening ray—
> I woke, the dungeon flamed with light.

That's God, and he is sending that out, and it is available, but God wants to be sought. That's where we have to come to our part.

One of the most frightening and important things for us to understand is how Jesus approaches us. In Matthew 13, Jesus is teaching in parables, and the question that comes from his closest followers is one we are apt to feel deeply: why do you speak to them in parables? Put it in other language, why don't you just run over them with the truth? That's what we are inclined to do as human beings, but it doesn't work, and it isn't in God's plan.

Jesus quotes these frightening words from Isaiah when he says,

> You will be ever hearing but never understanding; you will
> be ever seeing but never perceiving. For this people's heart

has become calloused; they hardly hear with their ears, and they have closed their eyes.

See, that's what they're doing now. The really scary thing is that God lets you do that. He goes on with Isaiah: "Otherwise they might see with their eyes, hear with their ears, understand with their hearts and turn, and I would heal them" (Matthew 13:14-15). You can almost hear the disciples say, "Well, isn't that what you wanted? Isn't that the best thing? What is going on here?"

God does not crash your party. He waits for you to wake up. If I am too absorbed in my own affairs, if I am too impressed with my own religion, too intent on bringing my truth as I understand it to the world, I will not seek him, and I will not seek him appropriately. I will do it halfheartedly. The promise is never halfhearted seeking. You will recall, he says, "You will seek me and find me when you seek me with all your heart" (Jeremiah 29:13).

When we are thinking about stepping into the kingdom and living there, it has to be something we want more than anything else. Jesus revives that message in Luke 14, as you will recall, where masses of people were hanging around him and benefiting from his presence, but they were not there for what he had in mind. They were there for their own benefit. They had their ideas about what should be happening and what God should be doing, and they were looking for him not only to help them, but also to manifest himself along those lines.

Jesus says these shocking words: "If you don't hate your mother and your father . . ." (see Luke 14:26). He goes right to the heart of most human life by addressing the family. The family is broken, and it tends to distort and misguide people. Therefore the restoration of family relations is one of the most important things that happens in kingdom living—to be able to honor your mother and your father. To truly do that is one of the things that I have found to be most difficult for Christians, and Jesus goes right to the heart of this and says, " . . . and your own life also, you can't be my disciple."

Now, there is a lot packed into that, but I think that is basic to the idea. If there is something else you have in mind, you can't be my disciple. You can't learn to live in the kingdom of God, and your eyes will be blinded. Again, I don't like to say anything critical of our churches and of the people who lead them, but if you look at what they spend their time doing, you might wonder what they are really about. You look at what they spend their time doing, and you are reminded of Jesus cleansing the temple and quoting Isaiah again, "My house will be called a house of prayer for all people"—all kinds of people (Mark 11:17). But praying is the last resort for most of our churches, though it is essential to living in the kingdom of God.

WHAT IT MEANS TO SEEK THE KINGDOM

Jesus is calling us to our part of seeking the kingdom of God with all our heart. That is our first priority: seeking the kingdom of God. Now, when you seek something, you look for it everywhere. If you are seeking your car keys, you look everywhere, and seeking the kingdom is like that. To seek the kingdom of God is to look for it to be present and for it to be an action, and then to identify yourself with that action.

Jesus says in Matthew 6:33, "Seek above all the kingdom of God and its righteousness" (paraphrase). Check your translation there. It is his righteousness, but it is talking about the kind of righteousness that characterizes the kingdom of God. Our first priority then is to seek that kingdom and its righteousness. Find out what God is doing where you are, and identify with it. Follow what you know to be the case, what you know to be true, of the righteousness of the kingdom.

Let's talk about how to do this. Many times people sing songs and talk all their life about seeking the kingdom of God, but there is no method to it. There is no how-to. You default to things like religious activities and perhaps a few other fragments of righteousness that you may have picked up, but not the whole story of God's presence and God's action.

Let's remember that God's kingdom is God in action. It's God reigning. It is the reign of God, but it is not static; it's active. It's what God is doing where we are. That is the kingdom that we seek. What is God doing now where I am? I am in a face-to-face relationship with an individual. What is God doing there? What am I looking at?

Dietrich Bonhoeffer, in the first chapter of his wonderful book *Life Together*, has a discussion of how Christians never meet one-on-one; they always meet under the presence of Christ. That's the way we escape the dreadful habit that human beings have of sizing one another up. Does that identify anything that you are familiar with? It's one of the most dreadful things in human life, and only the love of Christ and the presence of the kingdom can bring us beyond it. We meet a person—maybe it is someone we have known for a long time, maybe it's in church, maybe it's out on the street—and the first thing that happens is we have a program running about this person that covers their appearance and their demeanor and what they must be like because of this, that and the other. It breaks the possibility of meeting them under Christ in the kingdom of God.

I am seeking the kingdom of God when I am in a face-to-face relationship with another person. It doesn't matter if this other person is my enemy. I am given, under God, the ability to love and bring blessing to that person, no matter who it may be. The most important people are the ones closest to us, and that's where we can know the kingdom in a way we cannot know it anywhere else. It's in our personal relationships to other people. We seek the kingdom of God where we are.

Now, God has given us a lot of help on that, because it is only in seeking that we ourselves are pulled out of who we were and move to who we can be in the freedom of Christ. It's only in seeking.

CHANGE COMES BY GOD'S ACTION

One of the most abused passages in all of the Scripture is "a person in Christ is a new creature. Old things have passed away. All things have become new" (2 Corinthians 5:17 paraphrase). Now, there is sense in which that is true, and we should strive to understand it, but the way it is customarily used is false. We do not change quickly, and seeking is designed to pull us as quickly as we can stand it, with God's grace and cooperation, into a different kind of person. That means allowing those around us to become different, because we can't just bring it on them. They have to be given time. Seeking allows us to respond to God and God to respond to us.

There's a wonderful passage in 2 Chronicles that talks about how the nation of Israel sought the Lord at a particular time. The language is very valuable because it says, "and he was found by them" (2 Chronicles 15:4, 15). God isn't like the Wizard of Oz, who is waiting for us to find the curtain and pull it back and find him. No, God is active in this process, and we will not find him until he is ready to be found by us. Seeking allows us to grow and to change. It allows those around us to grow and to change. Seeking allows us to grow into people who can receive Christ into our lives and allows that to continue to grow until we reach the kind of fullness of Christ that characterizes the person who has learned how to live in the interactive presence of God.

Living in the kingdom of God is a matter of living with God's action in our lives. When we seek the kingdom of God, we are seeking more and more to allow God to be present in everything that we are and everything that we do, and we allow him to act and overrule and guide and help us become what he intended us to be. Seeking is fundamental.

Now, the key here, of course, is Christ. When Christ came and announced that the kingdom of God had drawn near and was available to all kinds of people, he was referring primarily to the presence of the kingdom in himself. It was in Christ that the kingdom became near and accessible, and it is through you and me that it becomes accessible.

You may recall that when Jesus later sends his people out, he tells them what's going to happen. They're going to be accepted and they're going to be rejected, but in both cases, he says, "Say to them, 'The kingdom of God has come near to you'" (Luke 10:9 NRSV). We are bearers of the kingdom of God.

RIGHTEOUSNESS OF THE HEART

Now I want you to put that again in the category of dignity, because your dignity and mine as ministers of Christ depends on the fact that we bear within ourselves the kingdom. We don't just talk about it. It is a presence that is in action, and our first step is to study Christ and to make him the one who fills our mind. The most important thing about entering and living in the kingdom is found in Matthew 5:20. If you don't know this verse, please study it and concentrate on what Jesus says: "Unless your righteousness exceeds that of the scribes and Pharisees, you will never enter the kingdom of heaven" (NRSV).

What does that mean? What is beyond the righteousness of the scribes and Pharisees? Basically, Jesus is talking about abandoning righteousness in action and moving to righteousness of the heart and the mind and all the spiritual aspects that make up the person, going beyond the righteousness of the scribes and the Pharisees.

Allow me to drive that home with his illustration: You no longer say, "I am right because I didn't kill anybody." No, the question is, would you have liked to? Or how happy or unhappy would you be if you found that person had dropped dead? Look at that marvelous passage in Matthew 5 that deals first with anger and contempt and then with the cultivation of lust or desire. These are ways of driving home the point about righteousness beyond that of the scribe and the Pharisee. That's very threatening, very hard, and in fact, it put Jesus on the cross in the end because of the opposition that arose from the righteousness of the scribes and the Pharisees. He did not conform.

It is interesting that much attention is given to things like breaking the Sabbath and hand washing and little food rituals. The battle in the Gospels focuses on those. When Jesus tries to turn it to things that really matter, the scribes and Pharisees go away and ask among themselves, "How can we kill this guy?" It is fascinating to see how bloodthirsty the people around Jesus were, but that's where the righteousness of the scribe and the Pharisee leaves you. It leaves you trying to manage affairs and make them work out as you think they should in your own strength, and so you need to have a little committee meeting here or get-together there and figure out how to get rid of this guy.

Beyond the righteousness of the scribe and the Pharisee is where we experience the kingdom. It's where we begin to enter interactively into the kind of change that allows us to live constantly in the action of God in our lives. As long as we stick at the level of action and of righteousness identified in terms of action, we will never move on to where the real action of the kingdom of God is. Of course, many people say, "Well, you're not very sophisticated." But that's why Jesus talked about children and said that unless you repent and become like a little child, you won't enter the kingdom of heaven.

You know, we have heard many sermons about how to do that, about how to repent and become like a little child. But that primarily means that we forsake the wisdom of men, of human beings, about how to deal with God. That's the primary part of becoming a child. A little child runs to the door, hears the garbage truck and says, "I want to be a garbage man." Mama and Papa hear that, and what do they think? *Hopefully he will change when he grows up.* But the direct and immediate enthusiasm for life in the kingdom of God beyond the righteousness of the scribe and the Pharisee is what is primary in entering the kingdom and living there.

We venture on Christ. That is how we come into the kingdom. The only saving advice, friends, is "Trust Jesus Christ." Don't just trust something he said or something he did. See, there are many people who believe in Christ, but they don't believe Christ. Further, they don't believe what he believed. But the progression into the kingdom is coming to believe what he believes, coming to trust it, to live on it, to act on it, to make it count. We do that by fixing our minds on him.

Now, you know, the old law will do a lot for you. Joshua 1:8 is one of the most important verses in the Bible. "This book of the law shall not depart out of your mouth; you shall meditate on it day and night, so that you may be careful to act in accordance with all that is written in it. For then you shall make your way prosperous, and then you shall be successful" (NRSV). Why? Because the law is designed to line you up with the kingdom of God. It's a great gift.

LIVING AGAINST THE GRAIN

That's what Psalm 1 is about. The woman or man in this psalm is feasting on God's kingdom. That's what the law is there for. It isn't there for us to make little tricks to jump through. It is to point us to the kingdom of God. If you set out to keep just half of the Ten Commandments, you will be thrown on the mercy of God immediately, because you will be crosswise of everyone else. But Jesus is the one who enables us to penetrate to the heart of the matter and sets us free from the obligations that have been imposed on us by ourselves, very likely because many times we impose stuff on ourselves as a way of getting along with others.

We say, "I'm going to be like this; I'm going to be like that." That's a deadly trap for those of us who are spokespersons for Christ, because we are constantly under pressure to please other people, and it will crush our soul unless we learn how to step beyond the righteousness of the scribes and the Pharisees and not be governed by what other people expect us to do and to say.

Be loving. Be kind. Be present. Accept others for who they are. Live with them there, but don't do what they say. Remember, that is what Jesus said about the righteousness of the scribes and the Pharisees. Do what they say, but don't do what they do, because they say and do not, and that is the deplorable human condition. The only escape from it is in the kingdom of God.

I will conclude with a verse that we know extremely well, but we need to dwell on it in the context of knowledge. Jesus was dealing with a bunch of people who were drawn to him, but they were not committed. He said to them, "If you abide in me and my words abide in you . . ." (John 15:7 NRSV). Now, the word *abide* is the same one that is used to talk about abiding in the vine. To abide in his word means to put his word into practice where you are, and that is the pathway to knowledge. He says if you abide in his word, you are his students indeed.

Something to Smile About

Now we are making the connection all the way back to becoming students. We become students in response to the message of the kingdom, and we start to grow. We learn about the easy yoke by experience, we observe the work of God with us as we go through our life, and we stop carrying the burdens. That's why the yoke is easy and the burden is light. Though the burden is huge and the temptation is to try to carry it, in the yoke with Jesus and drawing from the life of the kingdom you live with him. That's when the yoke is easy and the burden is light. So you can be the most cheerful person in town as a spokesperson for Christ.

You know, it's very telling that Mother Teresa of Calcutta trained the people who worked with her, and she would not retain someone who did not smile. They had to smile. Now, you can make that a life-crushing legalism, a frozen smile. But bless her heart—she, of course, did not mean that. She meant a genuine smile that comes from a realization of the goodness of God where we are, even if you have just been dragged in off the street and you are dying. You are dying in the arms of love. See? That's the kingdom of God.

If you put your life in his Word in that way, you really are his student, and you will know the truth. And the truth will set you free. It will set you free because it will be the realization of how things really are. There's a lot to smile about. *Joy* is the final word. "My joy I give you," Jesus said. Along with his peace and his love came joy. That is based on the reality that things are really better than you can ever imagine as you live in the kingdom of God. You learn that and you have joy. Joy is a pervasive sense of well-being that springs up in the cheer. I love that word *cheer*. We have associated it with cheerleaders and all sorts of silly stuff, but I love it when Jesus says in the old translations, "be of good cheer." That's where we live in the kingdom of God.

Conversation

Dallas Willard and John Ortberg

Dallas: Be of good cheer. Let's be of good cheer together.

John: That's a good idea. Most pastors ask as soon as the talk is done or as soon as the service is over, "How did it go? Do you think it went all right? Am I still doing okay?" I remember when you did a talk at our church one time, and we were walking out to the car in the parking lot, and you were singing an old hymn. It was like watching a child let a helium balloon go. I want that in my body, and I want that in my mind—the ability to do something and then just let it go. That's life in the kingdom.

Let's start there. You mentioned joy. One of my favorite games with you is asking you about a word, and you always have a definition. It's sifted through everything everybody has said from Homer on, and you can articulate it in a way that gets it right. It's part of why reading you can be so dense sometimes; every word is used with a precision that most of us don't have. So let's talk about joy. Why do you say that joy is a sense of pervasive well-being?

Dallas: Well, because it's consistent with terrible circumstances. One of my favorite passages on this is by Paul. When he is describing himself, one of the contrasts he uses is "sorrowful, yet always rejoicing" (2 Corinthians 6:10 NRSV). Joy is consistent with sorrow because it is a realization of what's really going on in the world at large under God. It's joy. You know, it's very difficult to think of God as joyous, because he's got so many things to worry about. But if you don't have a joyous God, you'd better head for cover. Really, you know? It's a joyous God that fills the universe.

John: I'll often think of joy in something else: a sunset, a child or something like that, but you tie it to a pervasive sense of well-being that, even in a difficult situation, joy is connected to that sense that I am okay.

Dallas: It's the ultimate word about God and his world. Creation was an act of joy, of delight in the goodness of what was done. Very often the most joyous moment for human beings is a creative moment. When they look back on it, they see the radiance of that moment, whether it's working on an automobile or painting something or whatever it may be. It's the act of creation, and you want to go back and look at it over and over again. I'm not much of a carpenter or anything else, but when I build something, I tend to go back and look at it pretty often. It's the creative aspect that goes with the love of God in creating. So it's really important to understand how joy cuts through everything and to anticipate that your moment of passage from the earth will be one of great joy.

John: Say a little more about that, about life and death, and life beyond death.

Dallas: Well, what Jesus teaches us is that within his presence and with his word, we begin to live in heaven now, and that's why he says that those who keep his word will never experience death, as human beings understand it. There is a continuity of life through what we view as death from this point of view, because we do see people die. Their bodies stop working, but they continue to exist as the people they are in the presence of God. I think many people do not realize they've died until later. Then they recognize that something is different. I love that line from John Henry Newman's old song "Lead, Kindly Light": "With the morn those angel faces smile / Which I have loved long since and lost a while." See, that's the continuity. Really, that's the continuity of life: live now, in the action and presence of God with his people.

John: Somebody just sent me a line this last week from G. K. Chesterton. At the end of his book *Orthodoxy*, he talks about how sorrow is inevitably a part of us right now, but never the most important part, and what is essential to humanity is joy because of the nature of who God is in life. But we live in a world that looks at it the other way around now; it is thought that joy is superficial and despair is deep.

Dallas: Right, and we have so many things pulling us away, and that's why Paul has to say in Philippians several times, "Rejoice in the Lord." Why in the Lord? Well, that's where you find the basis for joy, and so "rejoice in the Lord always: and again I say, Rejoice" (Philippians 4:4 KJV).

John: That's where the pervasive comes in?

Dallas: That's exactly right. Our part in living in the kingdom is to turn back to that and to keep Christ as fully present as we can and to thank God for his grace in helping us where we can't. We rejoice in the Lord. It's something for us to do. So it doesn't just sort of land on our head; again, this element of seeking, of participation, of cooperation is essential to life in the kingdom of God.

John: When you were talking about seeking the kingdom,

I was thinking that there is a way in which we seek joy too much or we seek the wrong kind of joy; we look to TV or just avoid unpleasantness. But then as you talk about joy, God and creation, it strikes me there is another part of us that doesn't seek it nearly enough or the right kind of it in every moment. That's part of why we don't love the kingdom as we might.

Dallas: Unfortunately, when people first hear about the kingdom—and this is very clear in the Gospels, and I've watched it for years—they think all their problems are going to be solved. They think of their problems as needing something to eat or whatever it may be. That's important. God knows, and Jesus was very gracious with providing food for people to eat. But that's not our ultimate need. Our great need is to see our place in Christ's world, in his kingdom, and to know that everything is taken care of.

We don't have a thing to worry about. But, my goodness, all the terrible things that happen—and you say, "Boy, I've got plenty to worry about. All these people have plenty to worry about." And I understand that, but that's not the solution. The solution is to acknowledge the presence of the kingdom in the most awful of events. Where was God in Auschwitz? He was in Auschwitz. Why didn't he do what we think he should have done? Well, that's a question to which I don't have an answer, but there is meaning to human history, including Auschwitz. God is over all. He will see to it that what is good and right is done, but you will always have to add the larger picture.

John: Come back to that question of practically seeking the kingdom of God. I remember talking about that one time, and a woman who was the mom of young kids said it was easier for her to seek the kingdom when she was single and didn't have kids, because they got in the way. She used to have a lot more time for quiet time. This is just one of the pictures of how we are restricted to certain activities in certain times.

This may sound a little strange, but in our work, what does it look like to seek the kingdom? At play, what does it look like to seek the kingdom? And you have said a little bit about sexuality and lust, and we so often talk about the dark side of that. And I don't mean to be glib, but what does it mean when a husband and wife are having sex with each other? What does it mean to seek the kingdom? How do you bring the reality of God, the presence of God?

Dallas: Well, to cover all of those cases, we realize that all that is good is God in action. That *is* God in action. Whether it is sexual or romantic relationship or play, God plays.

John: God plays?

Dallas: Yes. Creation was play for God, and so when we play, we can experience it—we see God in what is good in play. This is not an easy thing in a fallen world.

John: I never pictured God at play before.

Dallas: Well, again, it's a little difficult because we are not familiar with play. If you want to see play, you have to find a little child who has nothing to play with, yet is playing. Children never stop.

John: We would punish our child by putting her in the timeout chair when she was little, and she just sat there grinning. We finally asked her, "What are you doing?"

She said, "I'm thinking in cartoons."

Dallas: Well, that's wonderful. It's in the basic nature of persons to play, but it is very hard for adults to play because we are so serious about everything, about making everything happen and seeing to it that things come out right. We don't know how to play. Work is, of course, related to play, because they are both domains of creativity. Work creates value, and to be able to enter into that with God who is at work and to watch for him to move is a great part of life in the kingdom of God.

John: If work is creation of value, what is play?

Dallas: Well, play is creation of values that are not necessary. You know, you throw yourself upon the Lord, and you put yourself forth and you see what happens. Patrick Henry is said to have been a great orator, and he was described as someone who would throw himself in at the beginning of a sentence and trust in God Almighty to get him out at the end. That's creativity. That's really living in the kingdom. And in our relationships with other people at work or play or, perhaps more than anywhere else, in our love relationships, we need to have that kind of abandonment to God.

John: Do you have an image or language or question or reminder to help you in that? I know Frank Laubach used to talk about "games with minutes" where he would use a time frame to try to bring himself back to the awareness of the presence of God and his kingdom. But practically, are there things that you do to help you seek the kingdom in the different events of your day?

Dallas: Actually, I don't think so. I come back frequently and ask myself, "Now, are you doing this? What are you trusting?" This is especially important in church leadership, where we are mainly working with persons. Are you approaching this person in the presence of God—that is, not trying to control it? Are you giving your best to it, but your eyes are on God? I don't think I could say that I love Laubach's "games with minutes." It's a little like the Jesus Prayer for me. I can use the Jesus Prayer, but I can't use it all the time. Often I will substitute some other language, though I like to keep something running there.

I do think it's really important in the spiritual life not to be too controlling. That's one of the things I'm afraid that teaching about spiritual formation often falls into. It's a little more controlling than is really healthy. That's where the element of play would come in.

John: You have talked about dignity: the dignity of the easy yoke and the dignity of seeking the kingdom. What is dignity, and why is it important?

Dallas: Dignity is worth that has no substitute. If a thing has dignity, there is nothing you can substitute for it, according to Immanuel Kant. Most things have a price. That means there's a substitute. There's a price on a cheeseburger. That means if you give money to that seller, he will give you the cheeseburger. One reason we still have the blessed law that you can't sell human beings is because they have dignity. This is what C. S. Lewis is driving at in the greater *Weight of Glory*, where he talks about that. Bonhoeffer deals with the same thing in *Life Together.*

Every person has dignity, and when you see a person that doesn't realize that or doesn't associate it with their work in a society, where so often dignity is associated with work, you begin to understand why unemployment is such a terrible thing, and how it's important to understand that employment is not a job, though it may be a job. Employment is the creation of value. It's work, but it can also be play.

In the kingdom of God, we are set free to play—abandonment to God. Madame Guyon was imprisoned for years because of her religious views. She wrote a little poem about how she sat and sang in her prison and how she was content that God had placed her there. She retained her dignity because she retained her connection to God. That's what is crucial. That's what gives human beings the dignity they have lost, by and large, through alienation from God and through living in a way where others are attacked and they are attacked, and this process of evaluating goes on so ceaselessly. What a relief it is to be able to meet people without evaluating them, without sizing them up in some way. You can do that in the kingdom of God.

John: How rare it is for people to find a place that confers dignity on them. When I think of the word, I often think more of gravitas or somebody who is formal.

Dallas: Yes, that's how we have abused the idea. We think of it as something that is subject to human attitudes and control, and it's beyond all of that. We have to step out of that, and we do that by stepping into the kingdom of God. It doesn't matter how this person looks or what has happened with them or what they are thinking and so on. I meet them as God's creature. I meet them as someone God has a destiny for—a high destiny, higher than they could ever believe.

As spokespersons for Christ, it's so important that we carry this to people. There are many ways in which human beings have cut people down. We have to cut through all of that as best we can as we live and deal with other people. Also, I have failed so many times at it. My younger life was caught up entirely in this evaluation thing and so on. So, seeking allows you to be drawn out of that. It allows you to change, and you become different, and God cooperates with that project.

John: You said that in seeking the kingdom, you have to want it more than anything else. Say somebody says, "The honest truth is, I don't want it more than anything else. The honest truth is, I want to have more money or I want to be successful or I want to be loved by a certain person. If I'm honest about it, often I find I don't want it more than anything else. I can't flip a switch and make myself want it." So, what should people do if they find themselves in that situation, which I think probably all of us sometimes do?

Dallas: This is the classic position of Romans 7. We have so many different things going on in our lives and personalities that we can't master all the impulses. We have to go to the parts of the self and identify what it is that defeats us. Suppose I honestly want people to like me, and I want that more than anything else. Now, to deal with that, I have to go back to that with the Holy Spirit, with the Word of God, and I have to look at that. A major part of repentance is looking at things and seeing them for what they are. For the most part, that alone will begin to loosen the grip.

But we have to be willing to do that. We have to believe that it is safe for us to do that. Hopefully someone taught us that it is safe to do that, and then we can begin to break through as Paul does in Romans 8. We can come to the point where we don't greatly worry about what people think about us, for example.

John: Let's role-play that for a moment. Let's say we are talking with each other, and I say I realize that I really want that more than anything else. I want people to think well of me. How do you talk about that with me in a way that helps me?

Dallas: Well, we start with why you do that. What is it that makes you want that? We might talk about people that you know who don't want that and ask how they are able to function without it. I think if we do that, we begin to get an entrée into the dynamics of the self, which unfortunately the religion of the scribes and the Pharisees does not deal with.

John: I don't think our churches do, mostly. It takes time to do that.

Dallas: It does take time and returning to the question over and over. This is the process of discipleship. You see, this is what we can be doing in our group of disciples: finding out with one another what is driving and possessing us. I'm sure there are cases where possession has to be dealt with in a different way, but for the most part we are possessed by stuff that we haven't actually thought about. We haven't asked ourselves, "Where did that come from?"

That's what we have to do with the person who has said, "I don't honestly seek the kingdom above all." That's a big step forward. Then you can ask, "What do you seek and why do you seek it and how can you get back of that and release it by the grace of God?" All of this is by the grace of God.

John: It sounds like we have to find a way to get a lot more honest and open than we generally are.

Dallas: No, we just need to pause and hear it. We do need to find a way to be a lot more open and honest, but religion tends to make you closed and dishonest. Stepping into the kingdom means that we begin to feel the redemptive power of the kingdom moving into all of that and setting us free. The person who is closed and dishonest is manipulating other people for his or her own benefit. We have to know what that is and understand what drives it and absolutely go to God for help. And we have to use whatever devices will help us to overcome it.

In my thinking, this is a very orderly process. If you want to change something, you identify the disciplines that will help you do that. Sometimes they seem rather foolish. Perhaps the high water mark in this regard was St. Benedict, who, in order to escape lustful thoughts, threw himself into a briar patch. I think that would do it. Then you have to get beyond briar patches, because they are not always available.

See, discipline is again an area of creativity. Disciplines are not law. They are a venture. They are venturing on the reality of the kingdom. And we learn ways from others, and they set us free. So, all of this hangs together, and we just need to do it.

John: Most people do not have that association when they hear the word *discipline*.

Dallas: No, I know that's true. It's quite unfortunate that

Satan—if I may speak that way to make it simple—Satan seizes every word and twists it. He does that to spiritual formation. He has done it to discipleship, because in some evangelical circles, spiritual formation was introduced because the people concerned thought that *discipleship* had been utterly drained of its meaning, and it had, especially so far as its New Testament meaning is concerned, because it had become associated with particular things by good and well-meaning people, many of whom were sincere disciples of Jesus. Then discipleship became bondage to legalism, and so particular things like quiet times became a bondage, and they were not fruitful. They can be made fruitful, but you can't just grind away at something that isn't fruitful and make it fruitful.

I often tell people who come to me complaining about church, "Well, stop going." Usually that is enough of a shock to them. But we need to understand what going to church is about. It's a wonderful thing, and it can be a wonderful thing for anyone, but not if you go to figure out whether or not the performers are going to perform and everyone is going to be their churchy best. That raises the question I discuss in *Knowing Christ Today*: what is church meant for?

EXPERIENTIAL KNOWLEDGE OF THE TRINITY

John Ortberg

Thank you, God, that you care about us and that you made us. Thank you that you are always with us. We understand only a little, so very little, but it is what we want more than anything else, God. There has never been anybody like Jesus, and so we pray that you would make it so. How our world needs your kingdom to come! How our churches need it! How we need it! May it be so. We pray in Jesus' name. Amen.

JOHN ORTBERG

Ever wonder why there are people? Why there is history? Dallas says, "God's aim in human history is the creation of an all-inclusive community of loving persons with God himself as its primary sustainer and most glorious inhabitant." That's why there is history. That's why we are all here. God's aim is the creation of an inclusive community of loving persons, with himself included as its primary sustainer and most glorious inhabitant. Trinitarian fellowship and community run deeply in us, and that's why there has never been anything like the church and why stewarding the church is so important.

ONE CHURCH AND THREE PERSONS

Jesus has just one church, and this gets to a really deep part of reality. In Ephesians 4:1-6, the repeated word might be considered God's favorite word. The first verse says, "As a prisoner for the Lord, then, I urge you to live a life worthy of the calling you have received. Be completely humble and gentle." You might ask who these words best describe. Next, "be patient, bearing with one another in love. Make every effort to keep [or maintain, not create] the unity of the Spirit through the bond of peace. There is one body and one Spirit—just as you were called to one hope when you were called—one Lord, one faith, one baptism; one God and Father of all, who is over and through and in all."

The word that keeps coming up is *one*. God is three—the Holy Spirit and the Son, Jesus Christ, and the Father—and yet one. As I grew up in the church, I wondered how to best describe the Trinity. But the real question is, what's the significance of the Trinity? We might start with this: what do you think life is like within the Trinity? It is helpful to start thinking of the Trinity as a person, because personhood is so foundational to life and existence, and the unit of the person is indivisible.

What is life within the Trinity like? How do the Father and Son and Spirit experience one another? It's ironic that the most common argument among Jesus' disciples was, who's the greatest? There was an athlete years ago who was always associated with the phrase "the greatest." Muhammad Ali would tell the story of having a flight attendant come up and ask him to put his seat belt on. He said, "No, I won't."

She said, "Yes, everybody has to."

He said, "I don't have to."

She said, "You know, yeah, you do. We can't take off until you put on your seat belt."

He said, "I'm Superman, and Superman don't need no seat belt."

She said, "Superman don't need no airplane."

LIFE WITHIN THE TRINITY

What do you think life is like within the Trinity? Do you think there are a lot of arguments over who's the most omniscient? Who's the most omnipotent? Who's the oldest? The idea in the name is that it contains the character, the identity, the dynamics and the reality of the Trinity. We are talking about submersion in the name of the Father and the Son and the Spirit.

Consider the Holy Spirit in the Trinity for a moment. Dale Bruner wrote a wonderful book called *The Holy Spirit: Shy Member of the Trinity*. Of the Spirit, he said,

> One of the most surprising discoveries in my own study of the doctrine and experience of the Spirit in the New Testament is what I can only call the shyness of the Holy Spirit. What I mean here is not the shyness of timidity. Paul in 1 Timothy 1:7 calls him the spirit of power. It's not the spirit of timidity, but the spirit of difference. A spirit of concentrated attention on another. It is not the shyness which with we often experience of self-centeredness, but the shyness of other-centeredness. In a word, the shyness of love. The shyness of love.

There are a number of texts in the New Testament that speak

about the dimension of the Holy Spirit. Jesus said, "But the Counselor, the Holy Spirit, whom the Father will send in my name, will teach you all things and will remind you of everything I have said to you" (John 14:26). In other words, the Spirit will remind people about Jesus.

Jesus also said, "But when he, the Spirit of truth, comes, he will guide you into all truth. He will not speak on his own; he will speak only what he hears, and he will tell you what is yet to come. He will bring glory to me by taking from what is mine and making it known to you" (John 16:13-14). In other words, the Holy Spirit does not clamor to have attention focused on himself. His constant ministry is to get people to focus on Jesus.

Bruner said the ministry of the Holy Spirit can be kind of pictured like the illustration below. The Holy Spirit is saying, "Listen to him, look at him, pay attention to him, love him, follow him."

Figure 1.

Bruner says that the Holy Spirit constantly points to and gives glory to Jesus. But, he says,

It's often been said that the Holy Spirit is the "Cinderella of the Trinity," the great neglected Person of the Godhead. But the Holy Spirit's desire and work is that we be overcome again, thrilled again, excited and gripped again by the wonder, the majesty, the relevance of Jesus. The Holy Spirit does not mind being the Cinderella outside the ballroom if the Prince is honored inside his kingdom.

When we look at Jesus, we see that Jesus didn't walk around saying, "I'm the greatest." He said things like, "If I glorify myself, my glory means nothing." Jesus said he did not come to be served, but to serve. He submitted to the Holy Spirit.

All of the Synoptic Gospels talk about Jesus being led by the Spirit into the wilderness. Mark, who was probably the first among the Synoptic writers, said that the Spirit drove Jesus into the wilderness like you would drive a child. Matthew and Luke most likely did not include that because they wanted to keep Jesus' independence before us. Jesus submits only to the Father. As he said, "Not my will but yours be done." Jesus has this same shyness.

Then there's the Father. Twice in the Synoptic Gospels we hear the voice of the Father: once at Jesus' baptism, once at his transfiguration. Both times the Father said, in effect, "This is my priceless Son. I am so pleased with him. Listen to him. Pay attention to him. Love him. Follow him." It is worth noticing that the voice from heaven does not say, "Listen to me too, after listening to him. Don't forget. I'm here too. I'm the Father. Remember me. Don't get too taken up with my Son." God the Father is shy too. The whole blessed Trinity is shy. Each member of the Trinity points faithfully and selflessly to the other in a gracious, eternal circle of love.

I remember a Christian camp conference speaker a long time ago saying we're not supposed to be proud that God hates pride in people. That God is proud—that's okay, because he's God, and he has the right to be proud. But that's just one more case of us making God over in our own image. The reality of the Trinity is that at the core of existence, at the core of reality, are not protons or neutrons or quarks. At the core of reality is this circle.

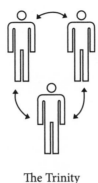

The Trinity

Figure 2.

It's the circle of Father, Son and Spirit. The Son submits to the Father, and the Father loves to glorify the Son, and the Son is driven by the Spirit, and the Spirit reminds everybody of the Son. The Father also sends the Spirit, and there is an endless, eternal, humble, gentle—all those words that Paul wrote way back in Ephesians—community. That's the Trinity with one another. That's what's real. That's the most real thing in existence.

HUMANS—IN THE IMAGE OF GOD

God exists as Father, Son and Spirit in a community of greater humility, servanthood, mutual submission and delight than you and I can possibly imagine. God is three, yet God is one. God is one, and then he makes human beings in his image. Genesis says Adam and Eve were two, and the two became one flesh. Two and yet one. See, being made in the image of God gives us the capacity for oneness, which is more beautiful and richer by far than a single person. The Trinity means God is never lonely. God never has a need. There is an enormous world of joy just within the Trinity, and then he makes us with that same capacity.

When Nancy and I were dating, we went on a picnic, and I quoted part of one of Shakespeare's poems for her:

So they loved, as love in twain
Had the essence but in one;
Two distincts, division none;
Number there in love was slain.

Nancy just looked at me with kind of a blank look.

The idea is that they loved each other so much that love in two parts had the essence of one. They were two distinct people, with minds, wills and so on, but no division: "division none;/ Number there in love was slain." There is a deeper logic here than mathematical logic. And so it is with the Trinity. "Number there in love was slain." They are three but one—and one infinitely richer, better, deeper, more joyful than it would be if not for the three.

COMMUNITY LOST

That's what we're made for, and we lost this in the fall and when we left Eden; that was all about the loss of community. If you follow through in Genesis, you see a little phrase that keeps cropping up: *east of Eden*. We end up east of Eden. For Israel, of course, to the east is where their enemies were. That's where wrongness and violence and hostility were, but we always long for Eden. We always long for that oneness.

Every time you see a great marriage, maybe you ache for that a little bit, or you see a parent and child that are really close, and you ache for that a little bit. We have this longing for union, and it will not be satisfied by match.com, by the greatest marriage, by school spirit or by a corporation. It just won't.

Out of this richness, God created human beings in his image. After the fall, the Son came to earth, and he prayed for his disciples, "My prayer is not for them alone. I pray also for those who will believe in me through their message." Of course, that's us. And then he speaks these amazing words: "That all of them may be one, Father, just as you are in me and I am in you. May they also be in us so that the world may believe that you have sent me. I have given them the glory that you gave me" (John 17:20-22). Isn't that just unbelievable? And that's not all.

> I have given them the glory that you gave me, that they may be one as we are one: I in them and you in me. May they be brought to complete unity to let the world know that you sent me and have loved them even as you have loved me. Father, I want those you have given me to be with me where I am, and to see my glory, the glory you have given me because you loved me before the creation of the world. (John 17:22-24)

And Dallas said,

> The advantage of believing in the Trinity is not that we get an A from God for knowing the right answer. The advantage of believing in the Trinity is that we then live as if the Trinity is real, as if the cosmos around us is actually beyond all else a community of unspeakably magnificent personal beings of boundless love, knowledge and power.

THE REUNION

Now, what cost does God pay for us to be part of this fellowship? Well, the Son says, "I will leave heaven and come to earth. I will disadvantage myself." This is love. This is part of why as Jesus says to his disciples, "A new command I give you: Love one another" (John 13:34). Why is it new? After all, that's an old, old, old command: love your neighbor. Of course, what's new is

Jesus. Now, in Jesus, we see God's love. He disadvantages himself so that human beings can enter into the trinitarian fellowship.

In some way that we will never fully understand, Jesus said, "I will leave the perfect oneness I have known for all eternity and become like human beings and take their brokenness upon myself, take their aloneness on myself, take their death upon myself, take their godforsakenness on myself." The Father says, "I will offer my Son whom I love beyond words. I will see him broken. I will see him rejected. I will see him killed. His pain will be my pain."

I have one son. I can't imagine that.

The Spirit says, "I will be poured out on earth in mostly silent and invisible ways. I will offer to lead and guide, never exalting myself, always pointing to the Son." To a large extent, the Spirit's promptings will be ignored or denied. The Spirit will be quenched. The Spirit will be grieved. The Spirit says, "This price I will pay so that anyone who might can enter into our fellowship."

We have been invited into the fellowship of love through the gracious ministry of the Holy Spirit at enormous cost to every member of the Trinity.

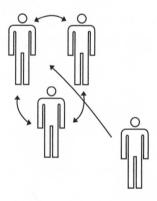

Figure 3.

Figure 3 is an illustration of the trinitarian fellowship, with us out here in our aloneness and our sin, and he says, "May they be in us."

ONENESS IN THE CHURCH

That's why Jesus says that when there is oneness in the body, the world will know: "May they be brought to complete unity to let the world know that you sent me" (John 17:23). It's not by accident that he says this, because that oneness, that community, is God's signature. He doesn't say, "May they be given the ability to out-argue all their foes." He doesn't say, "May they be given the power to change the culture." He doesn't say, "May they be given really cool worship services." Trinitarian fellowship is the foundation of the existence of that which is real. That's what we have been invited into at great cost. That's where we rest.

That brings me to the next wonderful statement by Dallas: "The Christian, the Christ follower, the leader, and the pastor, in particular, restfully and joyously serves in the midst of the Trinity in action as Christ builds his church." The pastor restfully and joyously serves.

All of us who are involved in church leadership have to decide who our main team is going to be. I may have a team that I lead as a department head, but then I sit on another team of the other department heads. Patrick Lencioni says that our main team has to be the team that we sit on with peers that are above us. Otherwise, we could just use our own team to aggrandize ourselves. But if a church, a community, a corporation or any group is not going to be siloed or be involved in turf wars and politics, the first team is the one that is above each of us.

If I'm a pastor, the trinitarian fellowship is my first team. My ultimate loyalty is to that fellowship. My primary identity is as a part of that fellowship. My understanding of how I am doing in life comes out of that trinitarian fellowship. No other team is allowed to determine my identity or evaluate my performance beyond that one. Am I serving restfully and joyously on a regular basis in the midst of the Trinity?

Several years ago my wife, Nancy, closed the door of our bedroom and said, "I want to talk to you." Then she got out a list. Now, she would not say it was a list. She would say it was just notes, but it had numbers on it, so I would say it was a list. She said, "When our marriage is at its best"—that is, like the trinitarian fellowship—"I feel like we serve one another equally." She reminded me of the early days of our marriage, especially when we had small children—a time when division-of-labor issues can be large in any family. It was easy for me to say I gave at the office. She would remind me that community intimacy is built on serving. It's not just getting stuff done; it's mutual servanthood.

She would say, "When I see you serving around the house, I feel drawn to you. When I see you vacuuming, I feel affectionate toward you. When I see you empty the dishwasher, I feel romantic toward you. When I see you bathing our children, I feel physical desire for you." I used to bathe those children three or four times a day. Come home late at night. "Hey, come here, kids. Get in the tub. Come on."

She said, "When our marriage is right, I feel like we are mutually the same, and I feel like that's kind of slipping. I feel like I serve, but our kids aren't seeing you partner. And I feel like when our marriage is at its best, we know each other equally. You know the details about my day, and I know them about yours. I know more about your work right now than you do mine. When our marriage is working right, there is a joy and a lightness to you. I miss that guy. I need that guy."

My initial response was, "I get it. I hear what you're saying. I miss that guy too. I just have to tell you, I have so much to do. I have so many questions that I don't know how to answer. I have so many problems. I feel like it's right here before me. So I want to live that way. I just need you to know I'm doing the best I can."

Normally when you say to somebody, "I'm doing the best I can," they're supposed to say, "Yeah, you got me there. I can't argue with that." But Nancy's immediate response was, "No, you're not doing the best you can at all. You could talk with a spiritual director about some of this stuff. You could hire an executive coach. You could talk to a counselor." She listed several things. "No, you're not doing the best you can."

And I realized she was right. I didn't tell her she was right for some time after that, but I realized she was. I was thinking, *At some point I will get this problem solved and this question answered and this deal done.*

LIVING EVERY MOMENT WITH GOD

But the kingdom is available now; I just have to want it more than I want anything else. The Trinity is right here. I don't have to wait. I don't have to be preoccupied. I don't have to have anything solved. In fact, I could say to the world, "Go ahead, bring it on, because nothing can separate me." I just have to want it more than I want anything else. I just have to say, "With God's help in this moment, I will refuse to allow anything to sever that from me."

At about that time, we had an extended time off, so I took a day to visit Dallas and Jane. We had a long talk. At one point, I asked, "Dallas, how can I help people in my church grow spiritually, because I would really like for it to be happening more than it is? What do I need to do?"

Dallas's immediate response was, "You must arrange your life so that you are experiencing deep contentment, joy and confidence in your everyday life with God."

My first thought was, *I didn't ask about me. I asked how I could help* people at my church *grow—what's the book they should read, what's the program we should put them through, what are the services we should have?*

He said, "The main thing that you bring the church is the person that you become, and that's what everybody will see; that's what will get reproduced; that's what people will believe. Arrange your life so that you are experiencing deep contentment, joy and confidence in your everyday life with God." That's not the elders' job, and that's not my wife's job, and that's not my friend's job, and that's not my congregation's job, and that's not my staff's job. It is not okay for me to wait until everything in my church or my world or my life achieves a certain level of resolution. That's life within the Trinity. If I want to move toward that, the outcome is a growing community of supernatural love in constant interaction with the members of the Trinity.

THE VISION

I think it was Gordon Crosby at Church of the Saviour in Washington who asked Dallas, "Why do pastors and church leaders end badly so often? They end up in a ditch, in a moral failure." Dallas's answer turned into a little booklet, another one of those that I have read a ton of times, and then as a chapter in *The Great Omission* called "Living in the Vision of the Kingdom of God." Dallas said that anytime somebody does something great for God, it always begins with a vision. But the vision isn't of what I'm going to do. It's not of what we're going to do. The vision is a vision of God and how good God is and how fortunate I am to be alive in God's universe.

That's the most important vision. It isn't what our churches are going to accomplish or how we're going to change things. When the vision is working right, I just keep coming back to it. My mind keeps returning as if it is returning to really good news.

Here's an example: A friend of mine in high school told me a beautiful girl liked me. I said, "I can't believe that's true."

My friend replied, "I can't believe it's true either, but it is. I have it on good authority."

That whole night, I could not stop thinking about it. I called her the next day, and it turned out it wasn't true. But I had one really good night when I thought it was.

A vision is that way. When it's working right, your mind can't let go of it. You keep coming back to it because it's so good. Again, that's what Jesus says: "To what shall I compare the kingdom of God? It's like a guy with a pearl of great price, a treasure in a field. The guy sells everything he's got in his great joy, so he can possess it" (Matthew 13:44 paraphrase).

Jesus keeps using money to describe the dynamics of the vision, because it's the simplest way for a fallen people like us to understand unforced desire. We have a show called *Who Wants to Be a Millionaire?* and the implied answer is "Who doesn't?" Who wants to be in the kingdom? That's what Jesus is asking. That's the vision, and out of that vision grows a desire to do something really good for God, just out of love.

Out of this vision are born remarkable outcomes. If we look at St. Francis of Assisi and John Wesley and others with the vision, we are impressed. And we think, *I'd like to be a part of that*. Then we begin to be a part of it, and the perspective shifts from the vision to the mission. We stop focusing on the vision of life in God's kingdom, and we start focusing on what we are doing. Then we have to keep propping it up, or else we start to feel bad about ourselves. Then we become preoccupied with methods and techniques and goals and measurements and outcomes. And burnout and stress and exhaustion are inevitable. And then sin starts to look good. The only antidote for this is to come back to life in the Trinity.

Church: The Original Human Community

In Disneyland is a ride called "It's a Small World After All." That song can drive you crazy by the time you get to the end of that ride. Where did that idea of a small world come from—the idea of no divisions, races, nations, people, tribes?

Once there was a man, and he taught about this. He said, "This is the core of reality, and I'm praying that people will come in." He had no money. He had no connections. He had no power. No office. Nothing. All he had were these words. He said, "Now I have prayed for this," and it started happening. People started to come in. People who had a lot of money got down on their knees and washed the feet of slaves. Nobody *ever* did that. Jews and Gentiles that once hated each other were like brothers and sisters. And they said strange things like, "In Christ there is no longer Jew or Greek, slave or free, male or female."

Thomas Cahill says that this was the first expression of egalitarianism in human history. It actually happened, and it happens still. That's why there's nothing like the church.

It's not just that there was never a community like this before Jesus. There wasn't even the *idea* of a community like this before Jesus. In the ancient world, there were guilds and there were philosophical schools and there were tribal religions and there were households and there were families. Community was his idea.

Now here we are, and we are stewards of this because it turns out that the foundation of reality is not a huge, cold, empty, dark universe. The universe itself is very small, and it's in the hands of the Father and the Son and the Holy Spirit—only three persons at the foundation of reality. It's a small world after all. Amen.

Conversation

Dallas Willard and John Ortberg

John: Talk to us a little bit about the Trinity, Dallas, because it's so confusing for a lot of folks. How do you think about the Trinity?

Dallas: I think it has been a threat to people because they've bought the idea that it's important to have the doctrine right. You know, we haven't had the creed that says you must get it all right, neither dividing the substance nor confounding the persons, and if you don't, you're headed for hell. I mean, what are we going to say about that? How many of us have got to the substance without division? Most people don't even have any idea what the classical definition of the Trinity means.

Now, when you add the tendency to say what really matters is getting it right, people don't know what to do, and they are confronted with the idea that you can have two that are one. Then they get balled up in issues about subordination in the Trinity, and then they read the Scripture, they read the doctrines, and they find out that actually the Father, Son and Spirit do different things. They begin to wonder about that and try to figure that out metaphysically and straighten out everyone's views on it. That's what makes people back away from talking about the Trinity.

John 14 is a marvelous portrayal of what happens when the Father and the Son and the Spirit come to live in us. Of course, that's what we want to be able to count on as

we are leaders, pastors, individuals or whatever—the
practical presence of the Trinity.

If we lose touch with reality and life, we'll never find
our way with the Trinity. We will always be at a loss for
what to make of it, yet people will say we've got to get it
right. You don't even know what right is. It's just hopeless.
So this becomes a nonfactor in the spiritual life.

You have beautifully presented what our life in the
Trinity is supposed to be like, and the John 17 prayer
brings this out extremely well. You understand that you're
dealing with the persons in this wonderful circle, who
don't care anything about their status. There's no subordination in the Trinity, not because of something meta-
physical but because the members of the Trinity will not
put up with it. They simply won't have it. So it's an eternal
Alphonse and Gaston routine: you first.

I love the old translation of Philippians 2 that says, "He
made himself of no reputation." That cuts to the heart of
everything so deeply. You think about Jesus hanging
around there in Nazareth, working with wood and unhappy customers, and helping to raise the family and all
of that. He had no reputation. Someone comes and asks,
"Where's Jesus?" And the reply is "Jesus? Jesus who?"

And the Father and the Spirit have that same attitude.
They have it because they love and admire one another so
much. People sometimes ask me what God was doing
before he created—as if he somehow didn't have anything
to do before he got us on his hands. I always say, "Well,
they were enjoying themselves together." Even in human
life, the deepest joy is when two people are able to be one.

John: I don't know how we can leave this without getting to a much more painful reality. Most of us here are part of churches. I work at a church. I love the church, yet there are times when I think about the church and the smallness and pettiness and mean-spiritedness and competitiveness and superficiality. Really it starts with me, but it is so mind-numbingly painful. And there's such a gap between it and the picture Jesus talked about. Why is it that way? Why is it so hard? What do we do with that?

Dallas: Well, I've thought and prayed and worried a lot about this myself. Once you back up and look at it, it's obvious that the separation between the churches in our communities is one of the hardest things to get past to begin to appreciate what Christ is doing in the world. I have tried to approach this by saying to ministers that the most important part of your ministry is that to other ministers. Come to know them, and begin to get over the idea of separation and competition.

Now, again, this is for spokespersons for Christ. Of course, ministers are central to this in many ways, but it isn't just the ministers; it's all Christians. The church in a community is not one of the churches. There are groups we can call churches, if we wish. I think this turns out to be very harmful, and you have to come to grips with usage and reality; it's hard to do anything about it, though people have tried to do that. They have given their church a different name—and usually they wind up being another denomination.

When I first went to South Africa twenty-five years ago, the Methodist Church there still refused to call itself a church. They had Methodist societies, which is good Wesleyan usage. When I went last time, they had become churches. It seems like it is almost hard to beat.

Individually we can do something. Individually we can know our fellow spokespersons, and we can make a point of making sure that there are some of them that are not like us. We can then begin to support them and pull for their success. Wanting other churches to succeed is one of the most important things we can do. Someone might say, well, but there's so-and-so, and gives a name. But that doesn't matter. We are disciples or we are nothing. As disciples, we love one another, and we care for one another, and we recognize the situation that we are in in a local community. We claim one another. It may scare the others to death until they get used to it, and they will want to know what you are up to. But with great relief, they will begin to understand that we are up to supporting them and pulling for them to succeed in God's terms. We can, I believe, make a start.

I think one of the reasons I am hopeful about what is now happening is that denominationalism generally has receded into the background of the spiritual life. When I was young, you could still sort of make a life out of being a Baptist or a Lutheran or a Presbyterian or something. It's very hard to do that now. Your identity in those terms doesn't mean much of anything, especially to the people on the outside.

We can begin to, in practice, assume that Christ and his friends, the Father and the Spirit, are building the church. They are building it where we are. We can begin to recognize it and speak and communicate and love across the lines, and contribute to the success in God of others who are different from us.

Paul says there's no Greek, no Jew, no circumcision, no uncircumcision, no barbarians, no Scythian, but Christ is all and in all. That's the reality. We just begin to assume it and act on it. I believe that God is breaking it down. I think what is appearing in our day is a growing realization that what really matters is not the divisions but what we have in common.

True ecumenicism is obedience to Christ. Discipleship leads to that. Christ's body comes together not by administrative actions, but by the actions of individuals who begin to step across the line and invest in the unity of the body.

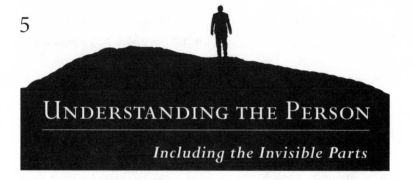

UNDERSTANDING THE PERSON

Including the Invisible Parts

Dallas Willard

Therefore go and make disciples of all nations, baptizing them in the name of the Father and of the Son and of the Holy Spirit, and teaching them to obey everything I have commanded you. And surely I am with you always, to the very end of the age.

MATTHEW 28:19-20

The deep, deep truths and realities of Jesus Christ are accessible to every person. We need to stand forth in the confidence that the knowledge of reality that we have in ourselves and that we bring to others in a gentle but firm, immovable way comes out of our knowledge of the reality of Christ.

Jesus said that if we continue in his word—if we buy it, if we really live in it—we are his students indeed, and we will know the truth, and that truth will liberate us into the greatness and goodness of God. I hope we can bring this to our churches, of all levels and all kinds, and that we can get past so many of the petty things that occupy our time and divide us from one another and give us bad reasons for not caring about one another.

After all, they are different in kind. But once we step into the area of discipleship, we are beyond that. Discipleship is the true ecumenicism. It's the way the people of Christ really come together, not by administrative action but by the spontaneous behavior of Christians toward one another. And this issues in a kind of obedience that is easy and routine because of the understanding of the reality of what we are dealing with.

Basically, we started out with the great verse where Jesus says, "Come unto me all you who labor." I believe he is talking about laboring under religion, and I think the context in Matthew 11 bears that out. He is saying, "Come to me and accept your life with me in the kingdom of God as a little child would accept it, and just begin to live it."

Teaching People to Do What Jesus Said

Then we looked at the Great Commission in Matthew 28, which spells out how you do that. Matthew 28 is what Jesus did. He made disciples, and he brought them together in trinitarian fellowship, and he taught them to do everything that he said. Now, by the time he left, there was a lot left to do, and there was a lot of growing to take place. That is certainly true today as well, when the main field for discipleship evangelism is in the church itself.

There are the people who are ready to go. If we will gently present the gospel and the reality of the kingdom of God in the context of the churches where we serve and the communities where we serve—and I realize church can take many different forms—we will see disciples emerging, and we will see people coming together in a trinitarian unity. Then we are in a position to teach ourselves and to teach others how to do everything he said. We occasionally need to remind ourselves that there isn't a single thing that Jesus said that we cannot do. There isn't a single thing that he said that we can do on our own, but we are not on our own. Everything that he said is accessible to us.

Let's explore the last phase of the Great Commission: teaching people to do everything that he said. The main thing to understand is that we can do that. It has to be intentional. It won't happen if we don't intend to do it. The sad thing today is that the bad news—the gospel of the devil, if you wish—is that you can't do it. But you can. Grace is here to make it possible. Grace is God acting in our lives to accomplish what we cannot accomplish on our own. The standard hackneyed definition of grace is "undeserved favor," but that doesn't tell you what it is. What is it? It's God acting in your life. What is God acting in your life? It's the kingdom of God. It's the reign of God in your life.

TRANSFORMING OUR PARTS

We have to talk in very particular terms about how change actually happens. There is one big thought that I want to make sure I get on your plate: if you are going to be transformed, you have to transform your parts. One of the things that defeats Christian growth is failure to attend to the parts of the person. For example, we have a statement from Romans 12:1: "I urge you, brothers, in view of God's mercy, to offer your bodies as living sacrifices, holy and pleasing to God." Now, that's an activity.

When I was very young, and Jane and I were together in college, there was a great man of God and medical doctor named Walter Wilson. He was the first person who ever said in my presence that we should present our bodies. Your body is one of the main parts of you as a person. You are a nonphysical reality with a physical body. That physical body is there for a great purpose. It's one of the things that differentiates you from an angel, and that's because God has a different plan for you and for me than he has for angels.

We are to present our bodies as living sacrifices, but notice the next verse: "Do not be conformed to this world, but be transformed by the renewing of your minds." So, if you wish to not be conformed to the world, one of the main things you have to do is transform your mind. And your mind, if it is transformed, will transform the rest of you.

That can be misleading, but we need to understand that we're dealing with a very complex being: a human being. That being has essential parts. Actually, they work differently in some people. This is important to understand, because when we come to the area of practical transformation, we're in the area of spiritual disciplines. Spiritual disciplines don't work the same way for everyone. Some people need more work on their body than they do on their mind, and others need more work on their mind than they do on their body. Some need deep soul work. Some are caught in a web of social relations that is simply destroying them.

We are going to look at the main parts of the person in a moment, but the idea here is very simple: take care of the parts, and the whole will take care of itself. Missing this will lead to a life of frustration. It will lead to a life of failure, because you'll keep trying to change you without changing your parts, and you can't do it. On the other hand, because that's the way things are set up, you *can* change you.

Look at a great passage like 1 Corinthians 13. When most people look at that, they despair, though they could become a person possessed of love. "Love is patient, love is kind." Most people get off the boat at that point. They don't want to go on.

"Love does not envy, it does not boast" and so on—all the way down to "always trusts, always hopes." And they just sign off. The same thing happens with the Sermon on the Mount, because they are thinking wrongly about how change occurs. In order to get this right, we have to think about the parts of the self.

THE ELEMENTS OF A PERSON

Each of us has within ourselves manifold sources of life. What comes out in the character and behavior of a person as a whole is an expression of a few sources in that person that provide the foundation for his or her life. Jesus gives us a list of these in Mark 12, for example, where he's asked, "What's the greatest commandment?" He doesn't say, "It's straighten up and fly right." He talks about the parts of the person. He says, "Love the Lord your God with all your heart and with all your soul and with all your mind and with all your strength" and "Love your neighbor as yourself" (Mark 12:30-31).

Think of this as a list of the elements of a person. Jesus understood that each one of these elements has to be dealt with in order to love God with all your heart, soul, mind, strength, and your neighbor as yourself. You can't just do it by will, for example.

Biblically, the heart is the will or the spirit. It is the source of creativity. It's power to originate. It is, I like to say, the executive center of the self. If you want to get ahold of what's going on in your life, you go to your heart. Jesus says you must love God with all your heart. To love God with all your heart is to have your will set on what is best for him above everything else. Love is the disposition to bring good to the object that is loved, and God has so disposed himself toward his creation—and his human creation, in particular—that we are able to participate in his life by setting our will toward what is good for him.

To love God with all your heart is to have your will and your spirit entirely set on the accomplishment of what is good for God. We often talk about a surrendered will. That's what the old hymn "I Surrender All" is about. It's being able to say, "There isn't anything in my life at this point that I would prefer over what is good for God." What is good for God actually isn't all that hard to figure out, because he has made a point in telling us, and our basic sense of what is good and right helps us understand that. The people who love God with all their heart are those whose will is totally devoted to what is good for God.

The mind includes both thoughts and feelings—the capacity to represent things. Your will depends on your mind, but interestingly, your mind depends on your will as well.

Each of these aspects of a person interacts with another. What is on your mind sets the scene for your will to choose. On the other hand, what is on your mind is a reflection of where your heart is. To love God with all your mind is to take your feelings and your thoughts and to devote them entirely to what is good for God. Your capacity to represent, to believe, to think and so on is entirely devoted to what is good for God. Because of that, there are lots of things that will never show up in your mind; there are lots of things you will never even think about doing.

One of the things that reveals character is what you have to think about. If you have to think about whether or not you are going to do things that are wrong, well, there's something wrong with your mind. You need to work on your mind, and that may be in the area of feelings or it may be in the area of representations. These go together. What you habitually feel is a major feature of your mind. It is tied to what you think about. So we have to look at what goes into our mind, and we have to turn that to the love of God.

LOVING OUR NEIGHBORS

People are relational beings. That's why the truth of the Trinity is so important for us to understand. We are not made to live alone, and we can't actually do that. But we have to be careful that our relationships to others are places where the love of God dwells. To love God, we must love our neighbor as ourselves. To do that is to inject what is good for God into all our relationships.

In a fallen world, human relationships are generally dominated by attack and withdrawal. We get busy sizing people up when we come in contact with them. We ask, "Are they going to attack us? Perhaps I had better be careful and withdraw before they have an opportunity to attack." That makes it impossible to love our neighbors. It makes it impossible for us to come out to them in the presence of God and manifest God's love in our relationship to them.

We don't attack people in the love of God. We don't withdraw from them. We accept them. We love them. Loving our neighbor is part of what goes into loving God. As John teaches us in his letter, you cannot love God and not love your neighbor. They don't fit together, because God actually does love your neighbor. It seems very unlikely to many as they look at their neighbor, but God does love them.

He loves the neighbor who is your enemy, so he very naturally says, "Love your enemies." To love your enemies means to seek what is good for them, in dependence on God. Of course, the best thing that could happen to your enemies is that they would come to know God, and our blessing on our enemies is designed to help them be in a position to know the God that we know. To love our neighbors is not to help them do the bad things they want to do to us. It doesn't mean to help them get their way, because very often the worst thing for human beings is to get their way. So we need to know how to stand in the world under God with our neighbor in an attitude of love.

THE BODY AND HABITS

The body is a little power pack that God has given us to live with. It works mainly by habit, and that's a good thing. Habit is a wonderful gift of God. In fact, spiritual disciplines are designed to disrupt bad habits and replace them with good habits. Habit is what you do without thinking. It also relates to what you do after you do something without thinking. The difference between Peter and Judas was what they did after they had done something without thinking.

Our body is designed to enable us to live without thinking. If you think that's bad, you ought to try to live thinking about everything. You would be paralyzed. You don't want to ride in a car with a driver who has to think about what he is doing. Hopefully, he is conscious. You can't always count on that, but you want him to be able to act without having to think about it. That is also true in personal relationships generally; we have to grow into good habits and out of bad habits to have proper relationships of love with our neighbors.

SOUL RESTORATION

The soul is the deepest part of the self. It is the integrative part of the human being. By the way, you aren't your soul, and your soul isn't going to go to heaven by itself. *You* are going to go to heaven. You don't save souls; you save people.

Because the soul is the deepest part of the self, you have to reach that part of you to bring wholeness to the individual human being. The soul is not something you have direct access to very often. Occasionally, if you're very quiet, it will show up. One of the main functions of Christian disciplines is to allow your soul to come out of its cover and to be recognized and re-stored. The restoration of the soul is fundamental to human redemption. "He restoreth my soul: he leadeth me in the paths of righteousness for his name's sake" (Psalm 23:3 KJV).

The law of the Lord is perfect, restoring the soul, Psalm 19:7 says. The law restores the soul by bringing it into harmony with what God is doing. As that happens, the whole person that has been divided by all the conflicts in his life and even in his own will is restored. The conflicted will is one of the most common features of the lost and fallen human being, but as the soul is restored, you're no longer defeated by the habits of your will. They are focused on God.

Sometimes the soul is so broken it requires special ministry. Indeed, all the dimensions of the self are areas where the min-istry of those who are able to act and live in the power of God is vital. Many people are so lost in destructive human relationships that they don't even know what is happening.

We have the great services of psychiatrists and psychologists who understand these kinds of things. Historically the divided person is the primary area where psychologists have come in to try to help put it all back together. Unfortunately, most of them have lost the idea of the soul and the idea of the person, so they are limited in what they can do to help. Unless they are Chris-tians or very wise people, they are limited in the resources they have to help people who are divided and whose soul is in trouble.

Now let me just say this: the Great Commandment of Mark 12 lists every dimension under the governance of Jesus' love. We have to make sure that when we are bringing ourselves into harmony with Jesus, we are learning to do the things that he said. That is a process of bringing all the parts of the person under his governance. Redeeming the mind and re-deeming the thoughts and the emotions is a major part of that, because they play such a role in determining how we choose and how we feel about things, and then how we act. This is where going beyond the righteousness of the scribes and the Pharisees that we talked about earlier becomes so fundamental; when we are working with these parts, we are moving beyond that righteousness.

Jesus often expressed his insights into this, and they are profound, of course. He often put it into figures like a good tree that can't bring forth bad fruit. He also says a bad tree can't bring forth good fruit. Given how we've been shaped by our thinking, we are apt to believe that last part, but not the first part. We are apt to believe that a good tree cannot bring forth bad fruit. So we won't cultivate the good tree, when that is exactly where the work needs to be done.

When you go back to the history of humanity and read Plato and Kant and all the others, East and West, who have tried to solve the human problem, you see that they come to this idea. You have to go to the depths of the person before you can begin to understand how goodness and godliness can come into life.

THE ROLE OF REDEMPTIVE COMMUNITY

You can't do this except in redemptive community. That redemptive community may just be your grandmother, and grandmothers often create some of the best redemptive communities on earth. It is people close to you. It is the churches, the ecclesia scattered through the community. When we go into these redemptive communities, we move into an area of restoration of the soul, restoration of personal relationships, restoration of our will, of our mind and of our feelings.

The message and reality of redemptive life comes in community. It comes partly because individuals are gifted by God with special abilities to discern and to speak to and to change things in a person that simply cannot be changed by his or her own efforts.

Sometimes instruction alone can help. Sometimes the practice of things like solitude and silence, service, Scripture memorization and other disciplines can do wonders to show people the single most complete discipline, which is worship, adoration of God. Those things can help, but we need the ministry of the body, and that comes through the gifts that Christ has placed in his people.

When we are thinking about church or fellowship, we want to think in terms of ministering in the power of the gifts that God gives his people and receiving that benefit to ourselves. If we slip back into the righteousness of the scribes and the Pharisees, we'll think only about running successful services, whatever that means.

The definition of *success* for the spokesperson for Christ is one of the most important parts of learning how to live in the easy yoke with Christ. Each one of us needs to think about what we take as a mark of success for our ministry. We need to understand how that always involves the transformation of character. Jesus talks about how some people will say, "Well, you've taught in our streets, and we listened to you. We can cast out demons, and we did works in your name." But he will reply, "No, I don't know you. I don't know where you're from." He has shifted the picture from the level of action to the level of character. Who are you? That's the question we want to have before us as we attempt to minister in the trinitarian fellowship.

Church can be the doorway to radical transformation. That's what we should expect and hold ourselves to by the grace of God—in all our local assemblies and all our gatherings of disciples. If we gather as disciples, that's what we will see—disciples who go through the process of transformation so they come out actually loving God with all their heart, with all their soul, with all their mind, with all their strength, and their neighbor as themselves. And you know what? Easy, routine obedience is what follows. That is the good fruit that comes out of the good tree. That's where we want to put our emphasis.

The last clause in the Great Commission deals with teaching others to do all the things that Jesus has commanded. Unfortunately, many people read that as teaching them what they ought to do, but it's talking about teaching them in such a way that they wouldn't think of doing anything else. As we do that, we begin to see the glory of the easy yoke and the light burden that Christ invites us to.

Conversation

Dallas Willard and John Ortberg

John: I think we are captured by the notion of change, and we hunger for change. Take the person who has been in the church for a long time, and they have tried to make some progress. But they find themselves saying, "I just feel change is so hard." People who talk too much have a hard time not talking too much. People who are fearful have a hard time not being fearful. Why is change so hard, and what would you say to the person who finds himself frustrated by that?

Dallas: Well, I would stick with him to begin with, because here the issue is a matter of details. The person who talks too much talks too much for a reason, and he may try not to talk too much. You try to help him find out why he talks too much. If he knows that and seeks to change, talking too much will take care of itself. That's the general pattern you want to look for.

In our teaching and leadership, for example, we want to encourage people not to want what they now want, not to think what they now think, not to feel what they now feel. Just go through the range of things. For every person who is concerned about changing a particular kind of thing, there is a reason they are troubled with it. This is absolutely vital in the habits that get so much attention, like pornography. Where does that desire come from?

You can't deal with these things by will. You have to figure out where they come from. Why do people want to do that? You often have people say, "Well, I'd like to give more, but I just can't." Well, why can't they?

John: Will you actually use that language and say, "You need to want; you need to not love what you want, and you need to not think what you now think"? Because that is a different aim than the person just starting to do the right stuff.

Dallas: Right. If you're not willing to not want, you're stuck. That's where the will comes in. If you are willing to not want what you now want, then you begin to find out why you want what you want. That requires fellowship. This is the kind of work we could be doing in our fellowships and in our small groups. I encourage groups to run a six-week seminar on anger and invite eight people who are ready to get out of anger. You could do it with lust or anything else, but get serious about education.

John: Have you done that in groups with people?

Dallas: I have done it with a group of three and have observed the change that comes simply from looking at where their behavior comes from. Now, you don't need to be very explicit about all this. You just need to do it. In general, in our churches and fellowship groups, we need to be very careful about announcing revolutions. We need just to begin preaching the gospel and encouraging people to come together and work on the things that they want to change.

John: How much would you say someone should expect to change? How much change, with God's help, are we capable of?

Dallas: You're capable of walking in all of the things that Jesus said to do. There isn't anything that you can't do by the grace of God if you are willing to go through the process of finding the roots of the behavior and changing the roots. If you are stuck on changing a behavior, you'll kill yourself, and everyone else will hate you, because you'll be a miserable person. You'll fail. They'll say, "Aha!"

But we can learn all the things Jesus taught if we go to the roots of behavior. Eventually, that means finding those areas of spirit, mind, soul, where the sources of the behavior come from. And it isn't just all negative. I wish I had time to talk about positive things like the great Psalm 119: "I have hidden your word in my heart that I might not sin against you. . . . Your word is a lamp to my feet and a light for my path" (Psalm 119:11, 105).

We're talking about knowledge. We're talking about learning what is the truth and living in that. When we do that positively, we're back to the Psalm 1 man. The Psalm 1 man's roots have gone down into the richness of the kingdom of God, and because of that, he brings forth fruit. The tree brings forth its fruit in its season. The mark of disciplined people is that they do what needs to be done when it needs to be done. I could probably take a score to Beethoven's *Moonlight Sonata* and pick out every note on that score, but I couldn't pick them out when they need to be picked out.

That's true in sports, tennis, basketball, whatever. The Lakers lost many series to the Celtics because a guy named Russell knew that if he could stay within five points of the Lakers, he could beat them. When it came down to the end, they would not be able to do what they needed to do when it needed to be done. It's the mark of disciplined people that they are able to do that, and often that means turning off what you're hearing and listening to another voice. But we learn how to do that always by looking at the details.

John: What would you say if someone is discouraged, ready to give up because they feel that change will never happen?

Dallas: First I would want to sit with them and listen to them and help them understand why they're saying what they're saying. My experience is that you don't have to go very far with that until people begin to see a light. You have to listen to people. We don't do enough listening. We think too highly of talking at people; we need to listen more. As we listen, we begin to perceive the roots of their behavior and find out why they are so discouraged.

Then there's an occasion to teach in that context—to teach not just by laying the truth out for them, but by saying, "Now, why don't you try this?" My vision of spiritual direction—which is not an educated one, just one that comes out of my experience—is that the spiritual director primarily helps people find ways of responding that will bring them in touch with the saving grace of God where they are. You suggest things for them to do, and then you come back and talk with them about that. That's how learning actually goes.

It has been my privilege to watch this in the lives of many people, often ministers. They are put in touch with reality that delivers them; it pulls them and gives them hope. The hopelessness comes out of trying what is hopeless over and over and over again.

As a young Baptist minister, I became conscious that

the best people in my congregation were the ones who felt the most guilty and would come and rededicate themselves if I put a little pressure on them. You know, as a Baptist, you can't get saved again, but you can rededicate yourself an endless number of times. They felt better if they did that, but that didn't solve their problem.

Sorry to inject so much of myself into it, but this is one of the things that really turned around my idea of how you minster to people. I realized I was not saying anything that was helping these people. That meant I wasn't actually helping them get into the things that were defeating them.

That's the key in all of these matters: You listen to people. You try to discern. Of course, this is a spiritual work, not just being clever; it involves intelligence and application. You listen to them, and you help them see why they're failing.

John: Sometimes people say spiritual discipline sounds like a purely human activity. You find out that somebody wrestles with gossip, and so if they practice silence, that might help them not to have to gossip so much. But, it's not clear, or they'll ask, "Where is the Spirit in that? Isn't that just human activity?"

Dallas: Well, it certainly is a human activity. Everything that goes into the religious life is a human activity. Going to church is a human activity. All human activities are designed to meet the grace of God. For example, the practice of silence can help you realize that you don't stop breathing when you stop talking.

John: When you say all human activities are designed to meet the grace of God, do you mean all spiritual disciplines or just human activity generally?

Dallas: All human activity generally, but when you come to spiritual disciplines, you have a special case with special needs that are being addressed. But they're all designed to engage the grace of God. We are built for that. That's what our creation was about, and that's what our work life is and our family life is—activity that meets the grace of God.

John: Say a little bit more about the soul. There is so much mystery around that one, and you've said that sometimes if we're really quiet, the soul will come out. How do you know when the soul has come out? What if the soul comes out and I miss it?

Dallas: I think that's a good question, because you're probably certainly going to miss it if you approach it in an attitude of anxiety. That's why the disciplines standardly give us indirection. That is, we don't try to find the soul, but we practice something that allows the soul to make itself known. The soul is experienced as a kind of inner force. I like to compare it to an inner river that pulls everything in our world together and makes our experiences one life. When the soul isn't functional, our experiences are shattered, conflicting, set against one another. We don't have integrity.

How do you know when your mind is showing up? Well, by experience: Now I am thinking. Now I am feeling. Now I am choosing. All of these dimensions of the self are learned by experience.

For the soul, we need people who can speak to us with some degree of experience and intelligence about it. We learn to wait on the soul and on God to come with the soul.

One of the things that happens in solitude and silence is you discover you have a soul. For many people, that's a big deal. They don't know they've got one. Their life isn't based on a sense of unity. Jesus asks a provocative question, which in English is translated, "What can a man give in exchange for his soul?" (Mark 8:37). What does it mean for your soul to be lost? It means that your life doesn't have a center that organizes your activities. You can't have that center until it returns to God, and God restores the soul.

People can help. Some have a ministry that is basically a soul ministry. A lot of what goes under the name of inner healing and healing prayer is soul work. It nearly always involves waiting for the Lord to make a context in which we can begin to be honest with what's in our soul. That's not a very satisfactory answer, but that's about the best I can do.

John: That's wonderful. How did you become aware of the fact that you have a soul? How did that happen for you?

Dallas: Well, basically through the realization that I was not a whole person. There was not an organizing principle that was drawing everything together and making me a whole person. Then I began to experience something of God's work in that direction in my life through some confession and some ministry by people who knew what they were doing with this. I began to discover there was a dimension to myself that I had not suspected. Jane was a part of this; after we were first married, we had some experiences with ministers who worked with people who were in desperate need of soul restoration. So it's a path of experience. You become aware of it. You become aware of yourself as being a part of a larger world.

Confession actually is very important to discovering your soul. It's one of the disciplines that really can be revolutionary because it goes so deep into the unity of the person. Essentially, when you confess you give up splitting the self.

John: So when you sin . . .

Dallas: You own up to what you are.

John: When you sin, are you always splitting yourself?

Dallas: Sin always splits the self to some degree, yes. You know that you have harmed yourself and others, but you probably are not going to come to terms with that because you're carrying on a charade of righteousness, even if you don't believe it. So confession is very deep in the process of discovering the soul.

John: Is that part of why, when churches experience the Spirit heavily, when there's revival, confession is one of the first signs of it?

Dallas: It's nearly inconceivable to me that you can have genuine revival without confession, because the breaking of the hindrances and the saving of face that goes into the charade of ordinary living is what has to be left to fall on the floor.

John: Why does it seem like people confess at Alcoholics Anonymous meetings so readily and at churches not much at all or not deeply?

Dallas: Well, AA got its start from the church. It is very sad that AA had to be invented to help people, many of whom were in the church, because they could not be honest about what they were living through. So AA drew from the sources of Christian teaching about these things. You can imagine the difference that it would make if we began our church services or our meetings together by saying, "Hi, I'm Dallas. I'm a recovering sinner." So much of our services are devoted to pretending everything is fine. We may have a little place where we confess our sins and receive absolution or something like that, but it doesn't go into the depth of our fellowship.

But AA isn't just the meetings. It's what goes into the relationships that come out of those meetings—the commitment of people to how they live with one another. Alcoholics Anonymous is one of the most brilliant illustrations of discipline and what it does on earth.

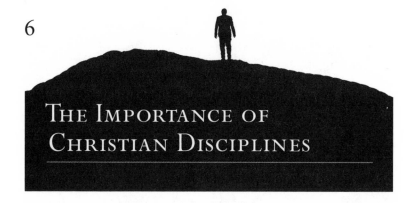

THE IMPORTANCE OF CHRISTIAN DISCIPLINES

John Ortberg

I have decided to follow Jesus;
No turning back, no turning back. . . .
The world behind me, the cross before me;
No turning back, no turning back.

"I HAVE DECIDED TO FOLLOW JESUS,"
S. SUNDAR SINGH

ow do we "do" life transformation? We must get into spiritual disciplines. I like to try to read Colossians 3:1-2 as if I've never heard it before and as if the writer is really serious about them and as if it expresses what churches are supposed to be doing: "Since, then, you have been raised with Christ, set your hearts on things above, where Christ is seated at the right hand of God. Set your minds on things above, not on earthly things."

DIRECTING OUR INTENTIONS

It's very interesting that Paul doesn't say, "Set your soul on things above," because the soul is not something that can be set. A will can be set. We can direct our intentions. A mind can be set. All of this language means something. Of course, "things above" doesn't mean "the way out there"; it means the kingdom. Set my will on the kingdom. Set my mind—now that's something I can do, because I have died and been raised.

"Your life is now hidden with Christ in God. When Christ, who is your life, appears, then you will appear with him in glory" (Colossians 3:3-4). I don't want to miss that. What will it be like when we appear glorious?

> Put to death, therefore, whatever belongs to your earthly nature: sexual immorality, impurity, lust, evil desires and greed, which is idolatry. Because of these, the wrath of God is coming. You used to walk in these ways, in the life you once lived. But now you must rid yourselves of all such things as these: anger, rage, malice, slander, and filthy language from your lips. Do not lie to each other, since you have taken off your old self with its practices and have put on the new self, which is being renewed in knowledge in the image of its Creator. Here there is no Greek or Jew, circumcised or uncircumcised, barbarian, Scythian, slave or free, but Christ is all, and is in all. (Colossians 3:5-11)

I always wondered what Scythians were doing in there. Scythians were particularly despised people. Replace *Scythian* with whatever people is despised in your culture; those are the Scythians.

> Therefore, as God's chosen people, holy and dearly loved, clothe yourselves with compassion, kindness, humility, gentleness and patience. Bear with each other and forgive whatever grievances you may have against one another. Forgive as the Lord forgave you. And over all these virtues put on love, which binds them all together in perfect unity. (Colossians 3:12-14)

Now let's go to 2 Peter, starting with the first verse.

> Simon Peter, a servant and apostle of Jesus Christ, to those who through the righteousness of our God and Savior Jesus Christ have received a faith as precious as ours: Grace and peace be yours in abundance through the knowledge of God and of Jesus our Lord.
>
> His divine power has given us everything we need for life and godliness through our knowledge of him who called us by his own glory and goodness. Through these he has given us his very great and precious promises, so that through them you may participate in the divine nature and escape the corruption in the world caused by evil desires. For this very reason, make every effort to add to your faith goodness; and to goodness, knowledge; and to knowledge, self-control; and to self-control, perseverance; and to perseverance, godliness; and to godliness, brotherly kindness; and to brotherly kindness, love. For if you possess these qualities in increasing measure . . .

That's a mouthful right there, isn't it? And that's kind of a big *if*.

> For if you possess these qualities in increasing measure,

they will keep you from being ineffective and unpro-
ductive in your knowledge of our Lord Jesus Christ. But if
anyone does not have them, he is nearsighted and
blind, and has forgotten that he has been cleansed from his
past sins. Therefore, my brothers, be all the more eager to
make your calling and election sure. For if you do these
things, you will never fall, and you will receive a rich
welcome into the eternal kingdom of our Lord and Savior
Jesus Christ. (2 Peter 1:1-11)

It hardly seems necessary to add anything to those words. We
could just live in that and then ask the question "Is my church
producing people like that?" That brings us to this question:
how? And this is where the spiritual disciplines enter in.

When I first read *Celebration of Discipline,* I did not like it
at all. I read it when I was in seminary, and my honest response was, "I already know I'm supposed to be reading the
Bible and praying more than I do, and I feel guilty about that,
and now some guy is going to say there's ten other disciplines,
so I have to feel guilty about those things too. Until I master
those, I can't feel okay about this thing called my spiritual
life." So I did not like that book at all, and I knew that I
probably should. I was going to seminary, after all. I was a
professional Christian.

When I got frustrated with my inability to change and then
read *The Spirit of the Disciplines*, I saw that authentic transformation is possible—because I knew I wanted it. It began to make
sense to me that authentic transformation is possible and God
wants it to happen. I knew there must be some things for me to
do; there must be a role for me to play. And that's where spiritual
disciplines come in.

TRAINING, NOT TRYING

In relation to spiritual disciplines, the most helpful distinction is the difference between trying to do something and training to do something.

Paul says,

> Do you not know that in a race all the runners run, but only one gets the prize? Run in such a way as to get the prize. Everyone who competes in the games goes into strict training. They do it to get a crown that will not last; but we do it to get a crown that will last forever. Therefore I do not run like a man running aimlessly; I do not fight like a man beating the air. No, I beat my body and make it my slave. (1 Corinthians 9:24-27)

Now, there's a role for the body to play, but the body is to serve greater purposes—my will and my mind and God—and not to be served. The body is a good slave. It's a very bad master. Paul writes, "I beat my body and make it my slave so that after I have preached to others, I myself will not be disqualified for the prize" (1 Corinthians 9:27).

Years ago my wife rented a movie featuring Sylvester Stallone that was set in the mountains. Everybody was wearing jackets through the whole thing, except for Stallone, who couldn't keep his shirt on. In all those shots, he's naked from the waist up, and he's rippling and bulging off the screen, with his massive pecs and deltoids. My wife looked over at me and then looked at the screen and then looked back me and looked back at the screen and looked back at me, and then finally said, "You know, I've just never been attracted to well-built men." I searched for the compliment that I knew was lurking beneath the surface, but it lurked too deeply.

Let's say that our challenge is to run, not walk, every step of a marathon. How many people would be able to go out and run a marathon right now? If we decide we want to run a marathon, what do we have to do first? We have to train. What does it mean to train? To train means arranging our life around those practices that enable us to do what we cannot now do by direct effort. The point of training is to receive power, so we arrange our life around practices through which we get power.

Even on what we call the natural level, transformation in any significant way involves training and not just trying. That's true for learning how to play the piano. That's true for mastering a sport. That's true for being able to speak a new language. And it is no less true when it comes to the spiritual life. Paul says, "Train yourself to be godly" (1 Timothy 4:7). And Jesus says, "A disciple is not above the teacher, but everyone who is fully qualified will be like the teacher" (Luke 6:40 NRSV). Of course, there is a close connection between a disciple and a discipline.

What Is a Discipline?

A discipline is an activity that I engage in to receive power. We tend to exaggerate what we can do through trying, and we tend to underappreciate what we can do through training. In many of our churches, we talk about Jesus and we talk about his love or his joy. People leave thinking they've got to try harder to be like Jesus. But trying harder does not work any better when trying to be like Jesus than it works when trying to run a marathon or trying to play the piano. Significant transformation involves training to do something—not just trying. Spiritual disciplines are training exercises to give us power to live in the kingdom.

Spiritual disciplines is a terrible term. The word *discipline* conjures up human effort and self-righteousness and a kind of military regimen. At our church, sometimes we talk about practices instead. As Dallas says, the devil always gets ahold of words and tarnishes them. And if we don't get that, we don't know what to do to enter into a Jesus-centered life.

People often mistaken disciplines for things they are not. Disciplines are not ways that we get spiritual brownie points for God. God is not sitting up in heaven with a little behavior modification chart, giving gold stars every time we read the Bible or pray or fast or confess. Also, spiritual disciplines are not necessarily unpleasant. We hear the word *discipline* and we think, *Man, that just sounds bad.*

Discipline depends on what you are training for. If you want to train to run a race, what discipline will you have to engage in a lot? You will have to run. If you are training to win a pie-eating contest, what discipline will you have to engage in? Pie eating. If every day you eat as much pie as you possibly can, a year from now you'll be able to eat much more pie than you could eat today. So, what counts as a discipline depends on what I am training for. If what I am training for is a life of love and joy in the kingdom, the way that I train will not always be awful, terrible, militaristic stuff.

Spiritual disciplines are not a gauge of my spiritual maturity. The disciplined person is not someone who does a lot of disciplines. The disciplined person, the disciple, is someone who is able to do what needs to be done when it needs to be done. The whole purpose of disciplines is to enable you to do the right thing at the right time in the right spirit, so if something doesn't help you to do that, then don't do it.

TRADE GUILT FOR GRACE

Because we tend to gauge spiritual maturity by devotional practices, we get guilty about them. My wife loves hearing that Jesus never journaled. The Bible is full of people who loved God, who lived under the Spirit, who fought sin, who grew in virtue, but they never went down to the stationery store and bought a little blank leather book and started filling it out. Now, if journaling helps you, if it helps to focus your mind as it does mine sometimes, by all means do it. If it doesn't help you, don't do it.

For God's sake, don't waste your time feeling guilty about not journaling or doing another discipline. We have more important things to feel guilty about. It's crazy that we can become people who are filled with judgmentalism and a lack of love and not care for people who are starving, and we don't feel guilty about that. But in the church, if I'm not journaling enough, I feel guilty about that.

We also don't compare disciplines against each other. We don't say, "Here's what you're doing and here's what I'm doing" or "You're doing more than me." We don't do it that way, because that's when it gets destructive.

Spiritual disciplines are a means to an end. This is where the relationship between discipline and grace is so important. In his book *The Cost of Discipleship*, Dietrich Bonhoeffer says discipleship is simply the reception of grace, and receiving grace is simply what discipleship consists of.

As a general rule in the evangelical church, we have been good at teaching people that they are saved—by which we normally mean their sins are forgiven so they can get into heaven—by grace. But we have not done a good job of teaching people how to live by grace. Living in the kingdom is just one moment of grace after another. I wake up in the morning, and instead of being burdened by all I have to do, my life is just a gift from God. My friend Jesus will go with me, and so I don't have to carry anything on my shoulder, and that's a moment of grace. Then when I see people, between me and them is Jesus, and so I'm kept perfectly safe by him, and I can love them. That's a gift of grace.

As Dallas says, we often think that it's sinners that need grace so much, because we have shrink-wrapped grace into the forgiveness of sin, but grace is way more than that. It is the power of life, and the reality is that saints burn more grace than sinners ever could. Dallas will say that saints burn grace like a 747 burns jet fuel.

How do we receive grace? Well, that's the point of spiritual disciplines. Disciplines are not the only means by which God changes us. We will have certain experiences; suffering is one of the primary ones. There will be moments—movements of the Holy Spirit in our lives or relationships with other people—by which we'll change. But spiritual disciplines are a fundamental way by which we are changed; in them, we receive grace. Paul says, "Be strong in the grace that is in Christ Jesus" (2 Timothy 2:1). And Peter says, "Grow in the grace" (2 Peter 3:18). The idea is not to grow in being forgiven for your sins. It's to grow in learning how to live by grace, to receive the power of God in your life to do what you can't do on your own.

Let's talk for a moment about spiritual disciplines and the fruit of the Spirit: love, joy, peace, patience and so on. We all know that we are called to live in those. Preachers preach on these, and those who listen often think, *I've got to try harder to be loving. I've got to try harder to be joyful. I've got to try harder to be patient.* But how do we grow in being loving, in being joyful, in being patient?

WHICH DISCIPLINES DO I PRACTICE?

Folks sometimes ask how I know which disciplines to practice. A really good way is to start by asking, "What would my life look like if I was living fully in the kingdom?" Then ask, "What barriers keep me from living that way?" Finally, ask, "What are practices through which I can receive power to be freed of those barriers and obstacles?" This involves working backward. You don't start by saying, "I'll do these really important disciplines," because it's about life. God is not interested in something called my spiritual life. He is interested in my life—the whole thing. Then he gives me gifts that are what John Wesley called "means of grace," conduits for grace.

We had moved to Chicago and our lives were very busy, and I called Dallas and described what life was like right then. Then I asked him, "What do I need to do to be spiritually healthy?" There was a long pause, and then he said a single sentence: "You must ruthlessly eliminate hurry from your life."

Then there was another long pause, and I said, "Okay, I got that one down. What else do you have for me? Because I don't have a lot of time, and I'd like to get as much wisdom as I can."

He said, "There is nothing else."

Hurry is the great enemy of spiritual life in our day. There's a difference between being busy and being hurried. Busy is a condition of the body having many things to do. Hurry is a condition of the soul in which I am so preoccupied that I cannot be fully present to God or a person. Jesus was often busy, but he was never hurried.

Now, how do you know if you struggle with hurry? Hurry in our day is actually hurry sickness, and there are ways to diagnose it. For example, consider your behavior. You're at a stoplight, and there are two lanes going your direction. There is one car in each lane, and it's a red light. You find yourself guessing based on the make, model and year of the car who's going to pull away fastest, because God forbid you should get behind the slowest car.

Or when you're at a grocery store, there are a couple of lines, and you count how many people are in each line and multiply it by the average number of items in each cart. If you are really hurry sick, you also do this: You're in line A, so you keep track of the person who would have been in front of you in line B. If that person is done and you're still in line A, you're kind of depressed, and you start to doubt the existence of God.

All right, so what do I do with my hurry sickness? Well, I can try hard to be patient—or I can look for practices. See, when it comes to spiritual disciplines, there is no set number of them. Anything can be an activity. For example, for a month, when you are on the freeway, drive in the slow lane on purpose. That'll kill you, won't it? When you go to the store, for a month deliberately get in the longest line. Deliberately. For a month, when you eat your food, chew.

THE EFFECTS OF A DISCIPLINE

A spiritual discipline is something you can do. It affects the mind and the body; it disrupts the normal patterns of thoughts and feelings that flow through you, which gives other thoughts and feelings a chance. That's what spiritual disciplines do.

This is why the self-help advice that you can choose your attitude is shallow. You really can't. You might be able to for a moment, but things like attitudes become embedded in our body. We badly need an understanding of the importance of the body in the spiritual life and what it means to have a body that can live without us thinking about what we are doing.

The will is very good at making big choices—to get married, to go to a church, even to decide that I will drive in the slow lane for a month. The will is terrible at trying to override the habitual attitudes embedded in my body and my mind. That's where understanding the parts and how the parts work and what the parts do well and what the parts cannot do is so important to have wisdom for how I enter into life in the kingdom.

One of the fruits of the spirit is joy. "Rejoice in the Lord always. I will say it again: Rejoice!" (Philippians 4:4). Joy is one of the great invitations and commands in the Scripture. Joy-lessness is a sin—a very serious sin. It makes the body of Christ unattractive to the people on the outside. It's a violation of the Spirit of our God and in defiance of his great gift: a pervasive sense of our well-being in the kingdom.

Let's say I want to be more joyful. What do I do? Well, again, in most churches, what most people understand is, I've got to go try harder to be joyful. But go back to the Old Testament, and look carefully. There are feast days, and people are invited to eat food that they love to eat and to drink things that they love to drink.

During one of the regular feasts described in the Old Testament, called the Feast of Tabernacles, the people in Jerusalem were to set aside a tenth, and then to "eat the tithe of your grain, new wine and oil, and the firstborn of your herds and flocks in the presence of the LORD your God at the place he will choose as a dwelling for his Name." Then it says,

> If that place is too distant and you have been blessed by the LORD your God and cannot carry your tithe (because the place where the LORD will choose to put his Name is so far away), then exchange your tithe for silver, and take the silver with you and go to the place the LORD your God will choose. Use the silver to buy whatever you like: cattle, sheep, wine or other fermented drink, or anything you wish. Then you and your household shall eat there in the presence of the LORD your God and rejoice. (Deuteronomy 14:24-26)

Can you believe that's in the Bible?

I grew up at Temple Baptist Church. We never read that passage at Temple Baptist Church. My parents never told me that was in the Bible. What's that about? Those feasts and celebrations are about training for joy. That's why feasts took up a massive part of Israel's calendar. Our world is radically unsuited to joy. So we must learn how to train for joy. That's why the last chapter in Richard Foster's *Celebration of Discipline* is "The Discipline of Celebration." That's training for joy.

Maybe you train for joy one day a week. One day a week, you eat food you love to eat and drink what you love to drink and wear clothes you love to wear and listen to music you love to listen to and do things you love to do and be with people that fill up your tank, because there are other people in your life who do not give you joy. They are like black holes of joy. They suck joy out of you like a Hoover. But on that day, you say to them, "I cannot be with you today. This is my joy day. I'll be with you again tomorrow."

We teach people that joy is a fruit of the Spirit. And we are to live in the Spirit and to grow in the fruit of the Spirit. How do we do that? Well, there are things that we can do. Our churches desperately need people who become spiritual doctors. That's one of the ancient descriptions for those who engage in soul shaping or soul craft or soul care—the cure for souls. It was understood to be very much like the cure of the body, where there has to be diagnosis and wise prescription and, of course, an understanding that only God can heal. Our world desperately needs wise, skillful practitioners of the cure of souls.

Solitude is another important discipline. In solitude, I deliberately withdraw from people, from work, from external stimulation. In *The Spirit of the Disciplines,* Dallas divides disciplines into two categories that I have found very, very illuminating: disciplines of engagement and disciplines of abstinence. Disciplines of engagement are things we ordinarily wouldn't do; they strengthen our doing muscle. With disciplines of abstinence, we refrain from stuff that we normally would do; this strengthens our not-doing muscle. For example, in study or worship, I'm engaging in activities. In fasting or silence, I'm abstaining from activities.

Historically, there are also two categories for sin: sins of omission and sins of commission. Now, sins of omission occur when I don't do things that I should do. My doing muscle is too weak. Sins of omission might include not loving and not rejoicing. If I suffer from sins of omission, I need to strengthen my doing muscle. I do this by engaging in things. So disciplines of engagement often help me as I wrestle with sins of omission. For example, I engage in celebration to help me overcome my joylessness and rejoice.

When I suffer from sins of commission, that means I'm doing stuff; my not-doing muscle isn't strong enough, so practices of withdrawal often help to strengthen that not-doing muscle. For example, if I have a problem with gossip, silence might be a very helpful practice. I was surprised early on, after I had read Dallas's *The Spirit of the Disciplines*, to find out that fasting actually helped me in the area of sexuality, because it was strengthening a muscle.

Spiritual disciplines are not about doing them for themselves. If we think that it is just about doing them just to become more spiritual people, we can do great damage, and self-righteousness becomes a huge problem. Always keep in mind that we ought to have both great devotion but also great freedom in the disciplines.

DIRECTION IN THE DISCIPLINES

Many, many years ago I wanted to learn how to pray, so I got involved in an Ignatian prayer group. We made a commitment, and we prayed each day and then gathered every week to learn. One of the men in the group came in one day and said, "I have now prayed thirty-two days in a row." Our leader, Sister Jean, replied, "Tomorrow, don't pray."

When I was growing up, nobody would have said, "Don't pray," as spiritual advice. I would have said, "Man, you could be like Cal Ripken. I'm not sure what the record for consecutive days prayed is, but you know, go for it." But Sister Jean recognized that inside him was a spirit of self-righteous judgment: "I've got my spiritual life in order, so why can't you do that? Why can't you pray thirty-two days in a row?" It was destroying the fruit of the Spirit in him. So the spiritual practice, the discipline that would most benefit him, was the discipline of abstaining from praying.

That's wisdom. As long as we understand what the goal and the means are, that will be really clear. But if we don't understand that, we just produce folks that are anxious and oppressed and obnoxious and weighed down. That's why Jesus said to the Pharisees, "You turn them into twice the sons of hell that you are."

As we go on the adventure of spiritual disciplines, there ought to be creativity and spontaneity and unpredictability, but also wisdom. We need doctors of the soul and folks who are doing this themselves and are able to help other people with it. Then there are certain practices that just by the nature of the human experience will always be important.

I asked Dallas one day how I know what to read, because I'm the kind of person who'll have stacks of magazines and books on my table—way too many. After another of his long pauses, he said, "Aim at depth, not breadth. If you get depth, you will have breadth thrown in. If you aim at breadth, you will get neither depth nor breadth." When we think about the spiritual life and spiritual practices, we must take into account human nature. The need for solitude will be a constant. If you get deeply into the writings of anybody who has progressed far with this—it could be Ignatius, it could be Wesley, it could be Calvin—those ideas get embedded inside you. When you go to read somebody else, you recognize, oh, that's what that's about. But if you just keep skimming from one to another to another, that framework never gets into your mind, and you never really get it.

When Alcoholics Anonymous was getting launched, there was a book about its origins called *Not God*. It came out of the Oxford movement, and as much as anything, out of Wesleyan Holiness roots. An Ignatian priest got involved with it early on, and when he saw the steps, he said, "Oh, this all came from Ignatius." But it didn't. Ultimately, it all came back to Jesus and wisdom about human nature and how transformation happens. If you are deeply immersed in any one person or tradition around disciplines, you'll recognize it when you go someplace else.

SOLITUDE: WASTING TIME WITH GOD

Because of the nature of the human condition, certain practices will always be fundamental. One of them is solitude. People often wonder what I do in solitude. Solitude isn't about what I do; it's about what I don't do. Solitude is a practice of abstinence. I deliberately withdraw from people, work and external stimulation to be alone with the Father. I eliminate all the scaffolding in my life.

We see this over and over in Jesus' life. At the beginning of his ministry, he spent forty days alone with the Spirit; and he went off to solitary places to pray (see, for example, Mark 1:35). Before he chose the twelve disciples, he went into solitude. After the death of his cousin John the Baptist, he went into solitude. He also did it after he fed the five thousand and after he sent the twelve on the mission. Things were going great, and you might think that was the time to really get busy. But he told his disciples to come away with him to a solitary place. He did the same on the night before he was crucified. Over and over and over, you see this pattern.

In solitude, I might meditate. I might study. I might pray. But what matters most isn't what I do; it's what I don't do. I just don't do the stuff I usually do. I don't allow my mind to be distracted, and then I find out what's going on in my mind. That's why you can't do solitude badly. When I decided to seek solitude for the first time, I thought, *Well, I will wait until I have a free day in my calendar, and then I will go do solitude for a day.* But I soon realized I was going to have to schedule it. I still have to be deliberate about it.

But then when I went to do it the first time, I had a list of things to pray for and was done in about half an hour. I had no idea what to do next. That solitude stuff was much harder than I thought. I was at Wayfarers Chapel in Southern California, and it was a beautiful spot, so I went down to the ocean and just sat there. It felt like an enormous waste of time. And that's not a bad definition of solitude: it is wasting time with God.

It's easy for me to think my identity is determined by how the people at the church think I'm doing. But when I go into solitude, I now can feel that leave my body. I think of the Father's words to Jesus, "You are my Son, whom I love," and all the *Is this going okay? How do others think I'm doing?* goes away. It's so temporal and so stupid how that hooks me the way it does.

In solitude, I'm free, and the disciplines are always about producing freedom. That's true also on the natural level: It frees a baseball player to make a great catch. It frees a musician not to have to think about the notes but just to make great music. If a discipline is not producing freedom in me, it's probably the wrong thing for me to be doing.

STUDY

In study, I immerse my mind in thoughts that lead toward the kingdom. Mihaly Csikszentmihalyi, a non-Christian psychologist, has done a ton of research over the last fifty or sixty years in a subject that he calls "flow." It's really all about consciousness. He was deeply influenced by a philosopher named Edmund Husserl, who Dallas is the leading expert on. He shares the conviction that consciousness is central to what it means to be human. Csikszentmihalyi says in his book *Flow* that "when left to itself, the mind turns to bad thoughts, trivial plans, sad memories and worries about the future. Disorder, confusion, and decay are the default option of consciousness." The apostle Paul says that the mind "controlled by the sinful nature" bears the fruit of death (Romans 7:5).

That's just the way it is it. Study is not about becoming an expert at biblical trivia. (We all know about those folks, and many of us *are* those folks.) It's about having a mind out of which flows a life of love and joy and peace, because it just looks that way.

HUMILITY

One of the great problems among followers of Jesus is humility. How do you pursue humility and try to be humble? C. S. Lewis said the result of trying to be humble is "Hey, look at me. I'm being humble." You can't do it by trying to do it, but you can by serving. When our kids were small, I'd practice servanthood on my days off. I didn't have an agenda; I would just be available. But even if I set out to do that, I would quickly degenerate to "No, what I want to do with my time is this." All of a sudden I would not want to be interrupted.

Servanthood as a practice can be a way to pursue humility without trying to be humble. Disciplines can save a pastor from being overwhelmed and a church member from despair about progress in the spiritual life, because they give us a concrete journey.

FROM INFORMED TO TRANSFORMED

Paul says, "Therefore, I beseech you, brothers and sisters." To beseech is to make an appeal. But an appeal to what? Think about the parts of the person. It's an appeal to the will. "I urge you." He's asking people to make a choice. "Offer your bodies"—there's the body—"as living sacrifices. . . . Do not conform any longer to the pattern of this world, but be transformed" (Romans 12:1-2). Really interesting grammar there. He doesn't say, "Transform yourself," but it is a command. There is something we're supposed to do, but we can't do it ourselves. It's a passive command, a passive imperative: "be transformed by the renewing of your mind." Yes, there's the mind.

Now, how do we do that? When they turned thirteen, I took each of our kids to a camp that Willow Creek had up in the Upper Peninsula, called Camp Paradise. It was very remote. It was very isolated. It was very Spartan. There was no decent furniture. There was no heat. There was no electricity. There were no lights. There was no running water. There was no indoor toilet. So the name was kind of ironic—Camp Paradise.

I would take each of our kids on the ropes course there, which was very interesting. Before we went on the course, we sat through a class that explained how the ropes work: here's the halter and here are the carabiners. If you use all this stuff, the ropes course is a perfectly safe place for you to be. We all listened, and we all believed. We all said, "Yep, that's exactly right."

Then I got up thirty feet above the ground on a rope ladder. The palms of my hands did not believe that up on a rope is a perfectly safe place for me to be. My armpits didn't believe either.

Here's the thing: I could sit in that class and listen to somebody give evidence that the carabiners and the halter would make me safe. I could sit there for a hundred years. I could repeat that talk. I could affirm it. But that would not change my body when

I got up on the ropes course. Information alone does not transform. It's indispensable—I have to have that information—but it is not sufficient.

There were kids that worked on the ropes course all summer long, and they had been transformed. They could stand up there, and their bodies—their sweat glands—believed that the ropes course was a perfectly safe place for them to be. They were free to think other thoughts and to feel other feelings, while the rest of us were not.

There was no mystery to it when we got up there: our minds were dominated by anxiety, our emotions were very unpleasant, and our bodies produced sweat. This was predictable. Just getting information alone wouldn't change that.

But we believe that if we just pour more exegetical and theological information into people, we've accomplished something. What we need is a ropes course for discipleship, so that, as Dallas would say, "We come to believe with our whole bodies what we say we believe in our minds." That's one of the ways to think about spiritual formation and the role of disciplines. We are coming to believe—the palms of my hands and our armpits are coming to believe—that the ropes course is a safe place for us to be.

That's why spiritual disciplines are an essential part of our strategy for teaching them to "do all that I command you." There's no way that we can do the ropes course of life, because that requires a transformed body and a transformed mind. The idea of presenting my body is I make my body available for spiritual disciplines, though I may be really bad at it.

The ropes course took about eight minutes to go through. One girl was petrified. It took her an hour and a half, and she screamed the whole time. She made it miserable for everybody else there, but she made it all the way through. She was a bad disciple. But here's the thing: if she kept going up to the ropes course every day, it would be just a matter of time. Transformation would win. It doesn't matter if the first time you do it you're a good one or a bad one. All that matters is that you keep doing it. You just keep going.

WHAT IF THE CHURCH . . . ?

The spiritual life is a domain of actual knowledge and reliable practice, and it needs churches. During one of the first times Dallas and I talked, I asked about the churches. Some churches are great at music and worship. Some churches are effective at evangelism or reaching folks outside of them. Other churches are teaching factories. Others are great at assimilating people. And still others are good at acts of justice and compassion.

But, I asked Dallas, where are the churches that are producing abnormally loving and joyful, patient, courageous people in inexplicably high percentages? I didn't mean places that have particular techniques or methodology. A concern that I have for the whole field of spiritual formation is that people tend to replace one set of methodologies for another, as if *lectio divina* is somehow more magically powerful than going through a Navigator's curriculum at Denny's at six thirty in the morning. God can use both of them, so it's not about technique or methodology.

What would it have been like to be in that little French church forty years ago when there was a young pastor named Richard Foster and a guy who taught Sunday school named Dallas Willard? What was God doing in that little church? I came out to California in the 1970s, and there were all kinds of great churches. When I was going to seminary, we visited around. Chuck Swindoll was there, and the Crystal Cathedral was there. And there was Hollywood Presbyterian and a lot of great churches doing great stuff.

But nobody was visiting that little French church. What if the work that Dallas has given his life to—recapturing the beauty of the kingdom in our day and making the pursuit of the with-God life and human transformation an accessible reality for ordinary people—what if it did not rise and fall with him, but became a river and then a great flood of life? What if, by the hundreds and then the thousands, men and women turned again to the living Jesus as their friend and teacher and guide and power? What if the experiential knowledge of God, and wisdom about the nature of the human condition and its transformation became the standard operating procedure in the church? What if pastors and teachers and small-group leaders and elders and those who lead little children in Sunday school classes were first of all devoted to and then found a way to make it available to all who are tired of life without the flow of grace? What if churches became schools of life? What if the angels ascending and descending on the ladder of heaven, and people from the surrounding community flocked to churches to learn how to live?

I know we cannot engineer or announce a revolution, but we have a part. I thought I would offer for me and for anybody else who wants to live in that vision to seek and to desire it above all. To pray and to ask God, "May it be so." Then to talk and to learn from each other.

Conversation

Dallas Willard and John Ortberg

John: Dallas, you have talked about your sense of the church being or possibly being at a point of decision. When you think about the future of the church, which you think about a lot, what do you think her future could be?

Dallas: The main thing that should and could happen, and that I think is happening, is that disciples of Jesus be conscious of one another beyond the boundaries of their local organization or assembly or however they identify themselves. When you look back at the emergence of Jesus and the disciples in the ancient world, the predominant fact is that the disciples were aware of one another, conscious of one another, supporting one another. When you read the letters in the New Testament, you see that standing out all over. The letters of Paul, for example, are to specific gatherings. One is to "the holy ones in Ephesus." Just Ephesus.

   I think that the main step in the move forward is that disciples become conscious of other disciples in their area of life. As that happens, there will emerge a different quality of fellowship, so that the mark of God in calling people out will be obvious and substantial in the lives of those who work at whatever businesses or church. This presence of God is the mark of what we have traditionally come to notice as revival. The manifest presence of God in an area will be the primary thing that we are looking for.

   Now, that's where we can do our part as spokespersons

for Christ. Again, it doesn't really matter what our official position is. But where we are, we begin to talk in terms of the body of Christ—that it is here and it is being built by the Trinity—and we encourage people to recognize, "Hey, what these people are talking about is the only way to live."

John: Dallas, how do we do that in a way that actually works? Sometimes in a city there might be an interfaith council or a gathering of pastors for prayers, and it's a good idea, but it almost never has that kind of life to it. How do we pursue it in a way that it doesn't become one more obligation in schedules that are full, but actually becomes a life-giving, breathing thing?

Dallas: The answer is that we arrange our time together so that we are actually sharing what is going on in our souls. We don't spend our time talking about community affairs or ecumenical efforts or comparisons between my church and your church, and so on. You have to arrange the time so that people are actually exchanging soul work that is going on in them, and they are sharing their experiences of the presence of Christ in his deeds and how they are learning and how their family is doing.

The really intimate things are where the work is done. I don't know that we can do that by ministerial associations. I'm a great believer in saying, "Oh, let them be whatever they are and be a part of it." Just don't mistake that for the real work. It's just like we don't want to mistake church services for the real life of Christ, but we want the life of Christ to be in our church services. And that's a wonderful thing. So it's a matter of watching the details of our lives and learning to be open and honest with other people, trusting, and seeking the well-being of other ministers and spokespersons for Christ and other disciples. That's where love comes in. Jesus says there's one thing that is the mark of a disciple: how you love one another. He doesn't say how you love the world. God's business is to love the world, and we should probably stay out of that—though we should care about the world.

Loving other disciples is the heart of the matter. Other disciples, we need to understand, are not partitioned out into denominational groups or project associations and so on. They're just human beings who are following Jesus, and we need to meet one another in that way. When we do that, all the wonderful things that we read in people like Bonhoeffer and others simply become real. Then you're onto something that will move of its own power, and all you have to do is be there.

John: How do we help people ask and answer the question "How is my spiritual life doing?"

Dallas: Well, very slowly, one at a time, we listen to them. "How is your spiritual life doing?" The next thing is a question and not a statement: "What's bothering you?" You start there. "What are you bothered about?"

John: When I was growing up in the church, if somebody asked how my spiritual life was going, I would have translated it to "Am I having regular quiet times?"

Dallas: Yes, there's a list that goes with each denominational group and tradition and so on that comes with answering that question, but the heart of the issue is beyond all the things you might list and categorize and so on. What you really want to know is how you and God are doing.

John: But you'd start with what's bothering you. That

would be an interesting liturgical question; start the church service with "What's bothering you?" And then the people could respond back, "And also you?"

Dallas: I think that would be absolutely revolutionary. It would be getting close to the AA model. That model doesn't allow you to start up with a bunch of folderol. You start out with how are you. Well, I'm a recovering sinner. So, how's your recovery going? What are you experiencing as hindering you? Then you listen to people talk, and you try to address those issues. Of course, it is important for us to say that this is a divine work. It isn't a technique. But we do need to do certain things, and we do need to not do certain other things.

John: It seems like in churches we end up either talking about theology that is fairly abstract or religious spiritual exercises for people to do that feel a little marginal. If we talk about life-relevant issues, it's really more therapeutic talk with a few Bible verses thrown in. But what you're talking about, which is actually life, starts where people really are in life, where it's very alive, it's very rooted in the concrete realities of our heart, our relationships and so on, but it is deeply tied to Jesus and to his way. We have a hard time doing that.

Dallas: Blessing one another is so rare, it becomes an official act, but we want to see if we can't get down to the intimate interactions of souls with blessing. We're so afraid to go there. I think that's partly because we are afraid we will be judged, and rejection is one of the most brutal things that happens to a human being. We don't say, "I reject you," but we do it. Our body language, our tone of voice and so on indicate rejection.

So we avoid that, and when we have a problem, we go to an expert such as yourself, a pastor, and you're supposed to fix it. But that doesn't involve you getting into the life of the person, which is the real call of the shepherd and the person who is in charge of souls. But the person who does that almost has to be naked. You have to be totally vulnerable to do that and to move into the area of need.

How can you become vulnerable? Well, you have to be prepared to live in the kingdom, and by that I mean to trust God entirely with what's going to happen here and now between me and you. Of course, that's the easy yoke and the light burden. We're back to that again. But getting there is our main problem, of course. If you could get a person to begin talking about what's bothering them—not what they think should be bothering them, but what's really bothering them—then you can begin to move into the area of the kingdom by your presence and your teaching and by learning to bless and be there in a way that you're waiting for God to act.

The important thing when I am talking with an individual is "What is God doing?" It's not about what I'm doing. I mentioned earlier Bonhoeffer's wonderful statement about how we never meet one-on-one. We meet with Christ over us, and when we do that, we are on the way to begin a fellowship. The first chapter of Bonhoeffer's *Life Together* is one of the most priceless, precious pieces of work you'll ever read. I don't know how an egghead like Bonhoeffer came up with this stuff, but he really had it. He didn't have off-putting scholarly stuff. If you think my books are hard to read, read some of his stuff, other than letters and papers. I mean, he was a heavyweight scholar of the most serious sort, and it's all good.

But he somehow was led by his experiences, and he tells you about some of those to the point where he turns it all loose; he says that when he meets with another person, he meets in the presence of Christ. What matters is not what we want or what the other person wants, but what Christ is doing with us. We learn to look to that, and that sets us free to be naked.

BLESSING

Dallas Willard

The LORD bless you and keep you;
the LORD make his face to shine upon you, and
be gracious to you; the LORD lift up his countenance
upon you, and give you peace.

THE AARONIC BLESSING
(NUMBERS 6:24-26 NRSV)

*A*s followers of Christ, we want to be points of constant blessing moving out to everyone around us. That doesn't mean we're talking all the time. Jesus promised that there would flow blessing from him through us. We do need to be able to engage that consciously.

Rather than just having a blessing in the sense that we stand up and put our hands over you and say, "God bless you," I want to engage you in blessing to a greater extent. If there is anything that I do as we go along that makes you feel uneasy or threatened, I want you to just cool it. Don't worry about it. We'll get through it. On the other hand, if you're willing to venture a little further than you might have in the past, I think you will find it a great help to understand blessing in a deeper way.

What Is Blessing?

Blessing is the projection of good into the life of another. It isn't just words. It's the actual putting forth of your will for the good of another person. It always involves God, because when you will the good of another person, you realize only God is capable of bringing that. So we naturally say, "God bless you."

You bless someone when you will their good under the invocation of God. You invoke God on their behalf to support the good that you will for them. This is the nature of blessing. It is what we are to receive from God and then give to another. The extent to which that goes is seen in Jesus' and Paul's teachings that we should bless those who curse us.

Now, a curse is the projection of evil on someone. It's using language or attitudes that project evil into their lives. We are to lay aside malice, lay aside anger, lay aside wrath. That's where we have to start: laying all that stuff aside, because it's already here. That's the nature of human life, and it's so oppressive and so hurtful. So then, how do we come back at it? "Bless and curse not." We will their good under the invocation of God. That's to bless.

Now we need to deepen that just a little bit, because it isn't just a verbal performance. It isn't "bless you" said through gritted teeth. It's a generous outpouring of our whole being into blessing the other person. So, among other things, you don't want to hurry a blessing. It becomes a habit that we say thoughtlessly, "God bless." Well, that's better than a lot of other things we could say, but we want to be able to put our whole self into our blessing. That is something that we need to be thoughtful about. We don't just rattle off a blessing. It is a profoundly personal and powerful act.

THE ART OF RECEIVING

One of the problems in blessing is to get the other person to hold still long enough to receive it. There is a great art and spirit to receiving a blessing. When we receive a blessing, we should not be thinking about blessing that person back. It is really a challenge to come to the place where you can just receive, and it's a part of the grace of life with others to be able to receive their blessing. I think we all feel very inadequate, and if someone wants to bless us, we feel we owe them something. But we need to move beyond that.

Blessing is an act of grace. It isn't an act of indebtedness. We just receive it, but we have to have time to do that. We have to be able to be calm in our soul to receive the blessing. One of the sad effects of how we give benedictions in our church services is that people are thinking, *When are we going to get out of here?* or other things. This isn't always true, of course, but they are apt not to receive the blessing that is given to them.

SHARING THE AARONIC BLESSING

In Numbers 6:24-26 we find the great Aaronic blessing. This is the blessing Moses instructed his brother, Aaron, to place on the people of Israel. Thank God for it! When you try to improve on it, you realize you are not going to make much headway. Let's look at this blessing and think about its content.

"The Lord bless you." That means "God bring good constantly into your life." "The Lord bless you and keep you." That means "God protect you. God build around you his safekeeping. The blood of Jesus and the Spirit of Christ be over you and keep you."

It's good to study this with the Lord's Prayer and with other parts of the Bible. Stop for a moment and think about saying that to someone: "God bless you and keep you." Imagine looking them in the eyes when you say it. This is very intimate and can be threatening. I've done this with groups where people broke out in tears and broke out in laughter because it touched so deeply.

Just think now about saying to another person as you look into their eyes, "God bless you and keep you." Emphasize *you*. This needs to be very personal. "God bless *you* and keep *you*. God make his face to shine upon *you*." There's so much about the face of God in the Bible. One of the most precious things that we can have is living before the shining face of God. Now, if you have trouble with the shining face, find a grandparent somewhere and watch their face shine on their grandchild; that can give you a little idea. There is such radiance that comes out of a person with the shining face. And your face is meant to shine. Glory is meant to be shared from God to human beings. Glory always shines. It always shines.

Now you are asking that God's shining face be over the person you are talking to. "The Lord make his face to shine upon you. The Lord be gracious unto you." *Gracious* means the flow of love and his activity in creating what is good. "Be gracious unto you." Again, don't hurry. Just go meditatively over it: "The Lord bless you and keep you; the Lord make his face shine upon you and be gracious to you; the Lord lift up his countenance upon you." That's interesting language drawn from how we relate to one another as persons. "Lift up" means something like, "May the Lord look right at you personally."

GOD'S PRESENCE IN BLESSING

This is about the manifest presence of God. We know that God is present everywhere, but he is not manifest everywhere. The invocation, the blessing, is designed to project that presence of God in a manifest way to the person you are talking to. "The Lord lift up his countenance upon you and give you peace." Peace comes in the presence of God, in having God's shining face over you and in having him looking to you.

The psalm says the Lord's ears are open to the righteous. His eyes are open to the righteous. His ears are open to their cry. To live in that atmosphere is what we're asking in a blessing. We're asking for an entire atmosphere of God's reality to be present on the person we are blessing under the invocation of God. So think of the depth of each phrase.

You can use other language; there's no doubt about that. But it's hard to improve on the language that God has selected and put on the record. He has said, "Now, if you use this, then it will accomplish my purposes in their life." So think about the depth of meaning in each phrase. We need to take time to think when we bless. We may have to grab the other person by the shirt collar and hold him to get him to stand still. We do this for children and for our loved ones and, as appropriate, for others that may come across our path.

BLESSING IN THE CHURCH

Think of the church as a place of blessing. Why do you go to church? To receive and give blessing. Again, you need a little time, and we need to make sure that there's enough room in our church service for God to accomplish something.

> The LORD bless you and keep you;
> the LORD make his face to shine upon you, and be
>   gracious to you;
> the LORD lift up his countenance upon you, and give you
>   peace. (Numbers 6:24-26 NRSV)

You may want to add some words of blessing, and that's fine. What is the good that you will to the person under the invocation of God? You may want to expand on that, and of course, blessing readily takes that form. If you are blessing and being blessed with someone who is a member of your family or close to you in many ways, there may be particular things that you want to add to the blessing. Remember, blessing is giving yourself and what is good to another person under the invocation of God.

You might want to conclude your services by letting the congregation bless the pastor. Or the musicians. Or the worship leader. It would be a wonderful gift to them to do that.

If you go through life giving blessings, it becomes a constant way of living toward others under God. We can take it into every circumstance of life. The more difficult the circumstance, the greater the need for us to bring the blessing, the benediction, into it. I challenge you to see the difference it makes. You don't have to say it out loud. You can, but you don't have to. If that is the atmosphere that you have generated, as you live in the kingdom of God, you're going to find it affects everything.

Learning how to do all the things that Jesus said becomes a part of this, because in the process of benediction or blessing, it is natural to do everything that he said. It gives you a place to stand when people around you are not doing what he said. It gives you a place to stand where you can be steady, and God will support you right where you are and enable you to do the thing that is good and is right. If you're having problems with that, remember to bring the blessing into it. You will find it is impossible to bless someone and to harm them at the same time. It can transform all of life.

BECOME A PERSON OF BLESSING

Imagine now becoming a person of blessing; imagine you and others being characterized by the blessing flowing out from you.

Our communities would be spotted with points of light from whom blessing flows. The church then would become an overwhelming presence in the community, and the love that flows in the community would become the testimony of the reality of Jesus and of God's plan and of the kingdom at work in us.

Imagine becoming a person of blessing. That's how you are identified. Think of someone saying, "Who is John?"—or Susan, or whatever your name is. And the answer is "Well, they are a person of blessing, and they think of themselves in that way." Who am I? I am a person of blessing. Blessing comes from me because God is living in me. I think of my own hopes, and I pray that you have received hope and inspiration as you have read this and that hope will rise up in you, and you will be a person of blessing and that blessing will surround your life because of the goodness of God.

I encourage you to experiment with the blessing in the intimate details of your life, in your church, in your community, in your business, at work, at school—just keep that blessing flowing.

Conversation

Dallas Willard and John Ortberg

John: Often when Jesus had a powerful encounter with somebody, he would ask them to do something afterward. That one thing wasn't a legalistic thing; it was a way to help them make it real and concrete and continual. With the rich young ruler, Jesus made a big ask: "Go sell everything you've got and give it away to the poor and then follow me." To the woman that was taken in adultery, it was, "Go and sin no more." To the lepers that he cleansed, it was, "Go and show yourselves to the priests." Then, of course, one of them went a step further and came back to say thank you.

There may be something you can take from this book that's between you and Jesus, that will help you go further, that will be concrete, that will involve a practice. It could involve a relationship. It could involve an event or a saying of thanks. It could involve finances or a person you would talk with or something at your church. Can you make space for that one? If it's not clear, you may want to ask, "Jesus, Lord, friend, is there anything I can do for you?"

Then take a moment to make a decision. Take a moment to be really clear, to say, "Now I'm deciding." If what you decided has a specific time frame, make a decision, a commitment, to meet that time frame. If it would help to tell somebody in order to make your decision firmer, do that as well.

Dallas, would you give a blessing?

Dallas: Almighty God, too one to be many and too many to be one, a glorious nature that we can only catch glimpses of by your grace, our hearts do rise up now in this moment in blessing upon you. We will your good, O God. Blessing and honor and glory and power be unto him that sitteth upon the throne. Our hearts rise up to you, overwhelmed with gratitude that you are and that you are who you are. We say bless you. Bless you, our Father. Bless you, our Savior. Bless you, Holy Spirit. Bless you, all in one.

May you rise above everything in our lives and hold us fast in the grip of adoration of who you are. We will and commit ourselves to what blesses you. On behalf of Jesus, we do that in this hour and ask that you would walk with us through life, that it should always be so, that our hearts would be rising up in blessing to you. So, let it be done, and we say amen.

ACKNOWLEDGMENTS

We want to thank all those who contributed to the work of putting together the "Knowing Christ" Conference, particularly, the film crew from Menlo Park Presbyterian Church:

Dan Baer, technical producer
Allin Chung, video technician
Dave Swartz, video technician
Rob Iriartborde, audio technician
Casey Fowler, media tech assistant
Scott Scruggs and Nicole Laubscher, social media

We also want to thank Erin Patterson, for conference organization.

Our appreciation goes to Carol Dunne for her faithful transcription of the conference talks to text.

We are grateful to the Dallas Willard Center, for providing funding for the "Knowing Christ" Conference and for promoting the work of Dallas Willard. And we are grateful to Jane Willard and to Bill and Becky Heatley for attending the conference and supporting Dallas there.

Gary W. Moon
On Behalf of Dallas Willard Center

Appendix

DISCUSSION GUIDE

Gary W. Moon

*T*his discussion guide offers a combined session incorporating the book text with the companion DVD. The content of the book and the DVD are the same, although the book has been edited a bit for print. You can use these discussion questions along with the book text without watching the DVD sessions if you prefer.

What other materials are needed for a successful small group?

- Television monitor
- Video player (stand, extension cord and so on)
- Watch or clock for monitoring time
- Leader's guide (contained in video case; can be shared in groups with rotating leaders)
- Bible—Old and New Testament (one per group member)
- Notepad and pen or pencil for everyone
- Book: *Living in Christ's Presence*

WHAT ELSE DO I NEED TO KNOW?

- This curriculum can work equally well in church and home groups. Each of the first six sessions can be experienced in approximately 120 minutes. The seventh session runs less than sixty minutes. In more formal, time-sensitive church settings, leaders will likely need to follow the time frames provided in the session outline closely to finish all the content. In less formal home settings, leaders can be more flexible. In either case, remember these are *suggested* time frames that can be adjusted as you see fit.

- It is likely that you will want to take thirteen sessions instead of seven to complete these materials. If you choose to do this, we suggest taking two sessions to complete each of the chapters, devoting one session to the lecture by either Dallas or John and a second session for the conversation or question-and-answer time that follows the lecture. The last session, chapter 7 (which would be the thirteenth session in this format) requires only one hour, so it does not need to be divided.

- Feel free to adapt each session to your particular group. Reword or add questions if you wish. If you sense a certain question is too inflammatory for your group or reaches beyond your comfort zone, simply omit it or at least recognize that not everyone needs to answer every question. Above all, approach these sessions with an expectant spirit that God will stretch the heart and mind of each participant.

Session One

HOW TO LIVE WELL: *ETERNAL LIFE BEGINS NOW*

Before you lead. For the best experience in leading your small group, it's very important to preview session 1 of the video as well as reading chapter 1. Familiarize yourself with the session outline and gather the necessary materials.

Session Outline.
Introduction (4 minutes)
   Welcome and opening prayer (1 minute)
   Question response (3 minutes)
Video Teaching (90 minutes; the conversation between Dallas and John begins at 44:05)
Video Discussion (12-15 minutes)
Closing (3 minutes)

> Note: You should be able to complete the session in either one two-hour block or two one-hour blocks.

Introduction. Welcome participants to the study, and briefly pray if you would like. You may want to say a word about the overall theme for the next six weeks and ask the group how they feel about taking the time to focus on the topic for this session: how to live well.

You may want to solicit responses from the group concerning the question "What does it mean to live well, to be well off?"

Video Teaching. Show the video segment for this session. Participants may wish to use a notepad and pen or pencil for taking notes.

Video Discussion. After the video presentation, explore the topic further by allowing the group to consider the following questions:

1. Dallas says, "When you divorce faith from knowledge, you wind up in the position of trying to get people to do things, not of providing them with a basis on which they can then decide how to live and how to lead their lives together." How would you explain the difference between faith and knowledge? (Hint: Biblically speaking, to "know" another person always implies intimate interaction.)

2. What do you think it means to pull rather than push someone into discipleship?

3. What is your gospel, your central message? (Hint: Is your gospel built more around an arrangement made or a relationship being lived?)

Note: If your group has decided to take two sessions to complete the first topic, ask the following questions after viewing the conversation between Dallas and John.

1. What does Dallas mean when he says, "The test of religious life is life"?

2. What needs to be true in someone's life for that person to be able to say he or she knows Christ?

3. How does having an intimate and ongoing knowledge of Christ relate to living life with a light burden and easy yoke?

Closing. Before wrapping up, encourage the participants to read and reflect on the following passages before the next group meeting:

- Matthew 11:28-30   Easy yoke
- Matthew 28:18-20   The Great Commission
- John 17:3   The only time in the Bible that Jesus defines "eternal life"

Close with prayer. Perhaps you'll want to lead in a prayer for each member to be willing to experience God's invitation to live now as his friend and student.

ADDITIONAL READING

Willard, Dallas. *The Divine Conspiracy: Rediscovering Our Hidden Life in God.* San Francisco: HarperSanFrancisco, 1998. (See chapter 1: "Entering the Eternal Kind of Life Now.")

Session Two

WHO ARE THE EXPERTS ON LIFE TRANSFORMATION?

Before you lead. Preview session 2 of the video and read chapter 2. Familiarize yourself with the session outline and gather the necessary materials.

Session Outline.
Introduction (4 minutes)
   Welcome and opening prayer (1 minute)
   Question response (3 minutes)
Video Teaching (64 minutes; audience question-and-answer session with John begins at 46:48)
Video Discussion (12-15 minutes)
Closing (3 minutes)

Note: You should be able to complete the session in either one two-hour block or two one-hour blocks.

Introduction. Welcome participants to the study, and briefly pray if you would like. You may want to see if anyone has a question from the last session's lesson and reflections, or you may want to say a word about the overall theme for this session: who are the experts on life transformation?

You may want to solicit responses from the group concerning the question "Did you have any experiences with easy-yoke living in the past few days? If yes, please say more."

Video Teaching. Show the video segment for this session. Participants may wish to use a notepad and pen or pencil for taking notes.

Video Discussion. After the video presentation, explore the topic further by allowing the group to consider the following questions:

1. Who do you know that is an expert in life transformation? How does one become such a person?

2. What are some of the differences between accepting Jesus as your teacher and accepting him as your Savior?

3. What would you most want to be said at your funeral? If all these things are already true about you, wonderful! If some of the statements are not fully true, what have you learned about how to become a genuinely good person?

4. How would you describe the difference between the gospel of Jesus and the gospel of minimum entrance requirements? (Hint: Feel free to quote Monty Python.)

Note: If your group has decided to take two sessions to complete the first topic, ask the following questions after viewing the question-and-answer session with John.

1. What is the real test of what a person actually believes?

2. What is the value of true belief?

3. If you were to develop a measure of spiritual maturity so that a scribe or Pharisee would not win, what item you would have on your test?

Closing. Before wrapping up, encourage the participants to read and reflect on the following passages before the next group meeting:

• Psalm 1	The two ways
• Mark 1:14-15	The gospel of Jesus
• 1 Corinthians 1:17-31	The shortcomings of human wisdom
• 1 Corinthians 13; 2 Peter 1:1-11; Colossians 3:1-17	What transformed (good) people look like

Close with prayer. Perhaps you'll want to lead in a prayer for each member to be willing to experience God's invitation to live in a conversational and transforming relationship.

ADDITIONAL READING

Willard, Dallas. *Knowing Christ Today: Why We Can Trust Spiritual Knowledge.* New York: HarperCollins, 2009. (See chapter 8: "Pastors as Teachers of the Nations.")

Session Three

HOW TO STEP INTO THE KINGDOM AND LIVE THERE

Before you lead. Preview session 3 of the video and read chapter 3. Familiarize yourself with the session outline and gather the necessary materials.

Session Outline.

Introduction (4 minutes)

 Welcome and opening prayer (1 minute)

 Question response (3 minutes)

Video Teaching (73 minutes; the conversation between Dallas and John begins at 40:55)

Video Discussion (12-15 minutes)

Closing (3 minutes)

> Note: You should be able to complete the session in either one two-hour block or two one-hour blocks.

Introduction. Welcome participants to the study, and briefly pray if you would like. You may want to see if anyone has a question from the last session's lesson and reflections, or you may want to say a word about the overall theme for this session: how to step into the kingdom and live there.

You may want to solicit responses from the group concerning the question "What does the phrase 'kingdom of God' mean to you?"

Video Teaching. Show the video segment for this session. Participants may wish to use a notepad and pen or pencil for taking notes.

Video Discussion. After the video presentation, explore the topic further by allowing the group to consider the following questions:

1. Dallas Willard says that the first step toward living in the kingdom is to study Christ and his gospel—the current presence and availability of the kingdom of heaven. Given that through Christ the kingdom is a here-and-now reality,

how would you describe your part in learning to live in the kingdom now?

2. Dallas suggests "ventur[ing] on Christ" and his teaching as the next step into experiencing life in the kingdom—the test of experience. What have been some of your experiences of living more and more moments with God? (Hint: Living in the kingdom is a matter of living with God's actions in our lives.)

3. Second Corinthians 5:17 states, "If anyone is in Christ, he is a new creation; the old has gone, the new has come!" What do you think Dallas meant by saying that this is one of the most abused passages in all of Scripture?

4. What is beyond the righteousness of the scribes and Pharisees?

Note: If your group has decided to take two sessions to complete the first topic, ask the following questions after viewing the conversation between Dallas and John.

1. What does it look like for you to be seeking the kingdom in your work, play and intimate relationships?

2. What is the best thing to do if you discover that seeking the kingdom is not your number-one priority?

3. Dallas has often said, "If you want to go to heaven, go now." How does that idea relate to living in the kingdom now?

Closing. Before wrapping up, encourage the participants to read and reflect on the following passages before the next group meeting:

- Ephesians 2:1-10; John 3:1-8   God's part
- Matthew 5:20-48; 11:25;   Our part
  18:1-4

- Matthew 6:33   Our first priority
- Jeremiah 29:13; 2 Chronicles   Why seeking is required
  15:4, 15; Matthew 13:13-15
- John 8:31-32   The path of knowledge for
                                  the disciple

Close with prayer. Perhaps you'll want to lead in a prayer for each member to be willing to personally experience God's invitation to live all of life as his apprentice.

ADDITIONAL READING

Willard, Dallas. *The Divine Conspiracy: Rediscovering Our Hidden Life in God.* San Francisco: HarperSanFrancisco, 1998. (See chapter 3: "What Jesus Knew: Our God-Bathed World.")

Session Four

EXPERIENTIAL KNOWLEDGE OF THE TRINITY

Before you lead. Preview session 4 of the video and read chapter 4. Familiarize yourself with the session outline and gather the necessary materials.

Session Outline.
Introduction (4 minutes)
    Welcome and opening prayer (1 minute)
    Question response (3 minutes)
Video Teaching (47 minutes; the conversation between Dallas and John begins at 34:12)
Video Discussion (12-15 minutes)
Closing (3 minutes)

Introduction. Welcome participants to the study, and briefly pray if you would like. You may want to see if anyone has a question from the last session's lesson and reflections, or you may want to say a word about the overall theme for this session: experiential knowledge of the Trinity.

You also may want to solicit responses from the group concerning the question "What difference would it make in how you live if you believe that you are created to live in a continuing, transforming conversation with the Trinity?"

Video Teaching. Show the video segment for this session. Participants may wish to use a notepad and pen or pencil for taking notes.

Video Discussion. After the video presentation, explore the topic further by allowing the group to consider the following questions:

1. What do you think life among the members of the Trinity is like? How does that vision challenge you as you live in communities of work, family and friends?

2. John Ortberg stated, "We have been invited into the fellowship of love through the gracious ministry of the Holy Spirit at enormous cost to every member of the Trinity." What are some of the ways you have found to live in a greater awareness of this reality?

3. On a scale of one to ten, how true is it that you are routinely restful and joyous in serving and ministry?

4. Share some ideas for arranging your life so that you are experiencing deep contentment, joy and confidence in your everyday life with God.

Note: If your group has decided to take two sessions to complete the first topic, ask the following questions after viewing the conversation between Dallas and John.

1. How would you describe to someone else what Dallas described as the "practical presence of the Trinity" in a person's life?

2. Read Philippians 2:5-11 (the "Hymn of Christ"). How should people go about imitating Christ in being willing to "empty" themselves (to use Dallas's translation) of the desire for reputation?

3. What are some practical suggestions for churches (and individuals) for getting beyond separation and competition?

Closing. Before wrapping up, encourage the participants to read and reflect on the following passages before the next group meeting:

- Ephesians 4:1-6   The unity of the Spirit
- John 13:34; 1 John 2:8   A "new command"
- John 14:15-31   What happens when the Trinity comes to live in us
- John 17:21-24   A growing community of love in constant interaction with the Trinity

Close with prayer. Perhaps you'll want to lead in a prayer for each member to be willing to experience God's invitation to *know* the Trinity as a community of love.

ADDITIONAL READING

Johnson, Darrell W. *Experiencing the Trinity.* Vancouver, BC: Regent College Publishing, 2002.

Session Five

UNDERSTANDING THE PERSON: *INCLUDING THE INVISIBLE PARTS*

Before you lead. Preview session 5 of the video and read chapter 5. Familiarize yourself with the session outline and gather the necessary materials.

> *Session Outline.*
> Introduction (4 minutes)
>   Welcome and opening prayer (1 minute)
>   Question response (3 minutes)
> Video Teaching (56 minutes; the conversation between Dallas and John begins at 34:49)
> Video Discussion (12-15 minutes)
> Closing (3 minutes)

Introduction. Welcome participants to the study, and briefly pray if you would like. You may want to see if anyone has a question from the last session's lesson and reflections, or you may want to say a word about the overall theme for this session: understanding the person, including the invisible parts.

You also may want to solicit responses from the group concerning the question "Of the five things you can do—think, feel, choose, behave and relate—which has been the most helpful to your own spiritual formation?"

Video Teaching. Show the video segment for this session. Participants may wish to use a notepad and pen or pencil for taking notes.

Video Discussion. After the video presentation, explore the topic further by allowing the group to consider the following questions:

1. Dallas states, "One of the things that defeats Christian growth is failure to attend to the parts of the person." He then references the admonition in Romans 12 to present your body as a living sacrifice. What are some ways that you have presented any of the aspects of you (thoughts, feelings, behavior/body, will, relationships) as a living sacrifice?

2. What do you think Dallas meant by saying that experiences of practicing the spiritual disciplines are not the same for everyone?

3. What does it mean to love God with your whole heart? (Hint: To love someone means to desire that person's good.) What are some things that would be good for God?

4. In terms of habits, what are the spiritual disciplines designed to do?

5. How does a person get to a place of easy, routine obedience?

> Note: If your group has decided to take two sessions to complete the first topic, ask the following questions after viewing the conversation between Dallas and John.

1. What does Dallas suggest should be done to help a person who has become frustrated by how difficult it is to change? Can you give an example of what this looks like in your own life?

2. What might happen if you become stuck on fixing or changing a behavior?

3. What are the roles of grace and the Trinity in the practice of a spiritual discipline?

Closing. Before wrapping up, encourage the participants to read and reflect on the following passages before the next group meeting:

- Mark 7:20-23   Where human failure and misery come from
- Mark 12:29-31   The Great Commandment—love of God and neighbor
- Psalm 19   Restoring the soul

Close with prayer. Perhaps you'll want to lead in a prayer for the group to celebrate the gifts brought by each component of our personhood.

ADDITIONAL READING

Willard, Dallas. *Renovation of the Heart.* Colorado Springs, CO: NavPress, 2002.

Session Six

THE IMPORTANCE OF CHRISTIAN DISCIPLINES

Before you lead. Preview session 6 of the video and read chapter 6. Familiarize yourself with the session outline and gather the necessary materials.

Session Outline.
Introduction (4 minutes)
    Welcome and opening prayer (1 minute)
    Question response (3 minutes)
Video Teaching (77 minutes; the conversation between Dallas and John begins at 56:48; note: You may want to view part of John's talk during your next session to balance viewing time.)
Video Discussion (12-15 minutes)
Closing (3 minutes)

Introduction. Welcome participants to the study, and briefly pray if you would like. You may want to see if anyone has a question from the last session's lesson and reflections, or you may want to say a word about the overall theme for this session: the importance of Christian disciplines.

You also may want to solicit responses from the group concerning the question "What is the current role of Christian disciplines in your life?"

Video Teaching. Show the video segment for this session. Participants may wish to use a notepad and pen or pencil for taking notes.

Video Discussion. After the video presentation, explore the topic further by allowing the group to consider the following questions:

1. After listening to John Ortberg's reading of Colossians 3:1-14 and 2 Peter 1:1-11, are there any practices you have found to be helpful for making these verses a reality in your life?

2. When it comes to authentic Christian spiritual formation, how would you explain the difference between training and trying?

3. If *any* activity has the potential to be a spiritual discipline for a person (such as purposefully driving in the slow lane), what are some activities that could become a spiritual discipline in your life? Is the activity a discipline of abstinence or engagement?

Note: If your group has decided to take two sessions to complete the first topic, ask the following questions after viewing the conversation between Dallas and John.

1. What is your plan for becoming more aware of other disciples (apprentices to Jesus) in your area? How can you encourage each other in practical ways?

2. If discipleship is, as Dietrich Bonhoeffer described, simply the reception of grace, how can a spiritual discipline play a role in receiving grace?

3. What is bothering you?

Closing. Before wrapping up, encourage the participants to read and reflect on the following passages before the next group meeting:

• Colossians 3:1-14; 2 Peter 1:1-11	Exercising responsibility for who we become
• 1 Corinthians 9:24	Training versus trying
• Galatians 5:22-25	Spiritual disciplines and the fruit of the Spirit

Close with prayer. Perhaps you'll want to lead in a prayer for each member to be willing to find ways of arranging life to form new life-giving habits.

ADDITIONAL READING

Willard, Dallas. *The Spirit of the Disciplines.* San Francisco: Harper & Row, 1988.

Session Seven

BLESSING

Before you lead. Preview session 7 of the video and read chapter 7. Familiarize yourself with the session outline and gather the necessary materials.

Session Outline.

Introduction (4 minutes)

   Welcome and opening prayer (1 minute)

   Question response (3 minutes)

Video Teaching (24 minutes; present this recording in one session)

Video Discussion (12-15 minutes)

Closing (3 minutes)

Introduction. Welcome participants to the study, and briefly pray if you would like. You may want to see if anyone has a question from the last session's lesson and reflections, or you may want to say a word about the overall theme for this session: blessing.

You also may want to solicit responses from the group to the following: "Describe a time when you have received a blessing from another person that had a healing effect on your soul."

Video Teaching. Show the video segment for this session. Participants may wish to use a notepad and pen or pencil for taking notes.

Video Discussion. After the video presentation, explore the topic further by allowing the group to consider the following questions:

1. How would you explain the difference between a blessing and a curse?

2. What do you mean when you say to another person, "God bless you"?

3. Have you ever had the sense of God looking right at you?

Closing. Encourage the participants to pair into groups of two and to bless each other with the Aaronic blessing:

The LORD bless you and keep you;
the LORD make his face to shine upon you, and be
    gracious to you;
the LORD lift up his countenance upon you, and give you
    peace. (Numbers 6:24-26 NRSV)

Close with prayer. Perhaps you'll want to lead in a slow reading of Dallas's paraphrasing of the Lord's Prayer (from *The Divine Conspiracy* [San Francisco: HarperSanFrancisco, 1998], p. 269):

Dear Father always near us,
may your name be treasured and loved,
may your rule be completed in us,
may your will be done here on earth in just the way it is
    done in heaven.
Give us today the things we need today,
and forgive us our sins and impositions on you
as we are forgiving all who in any way offend us.
Please don't put us through trials,
but deliver us from everything bad.
Because you are the one in charge,
and you have all the power,
and the glory too is all yours—forever.
Which is just the way we want it!

ADDITIONAL READING

Willard, Dallas. *The Great Omission.* San Francisco: Harper &
Row, 2006.

DALLAS WILLARD CENTER *for* CHRISTIAN SPIRITUAL FORMATION
WESTMONT COLLEGE

The Dallas Willard Center is dedicated to placing an enduring emphasis on the intellectual legacy of Dallas Willard, including his focus on the possibility and path to authentic spiritual and moral transformation. The Dallas Willard Center exists under the broader umbrella of the Martin Institute for Christianity and Culture.

Goals

The goals of the Martin Institute and Dallas Willard Center include:

- Creation of a new generation of individuals who will become thought leaders in articulating and experiencing an interactive relationship with Jesus Christ.

- Support the establishment of the field of Christian spiritual formation as a discipline of public knowledge that is open to research and pedagogy of the highest order.

The work of the Martin Institute and Dallas Willard Center is focused on three primary areas:

On-Campus Formation

The Martin Institute and Dallas Willard Center is working alongside the academic and student life departments at Westmont College to pilot a variety of spiritual formation programs and opportunities for students.

Research

The Martin Institute and Dallas Willard Center desires to support and engage in Christian spiritual formation research and writing efforts and to develop an online collection of materials accessible to researchers and other visitors. Early program initiatives include a senior fellows program, annual book and research awards, and online research.

Resource Development

The Martin Institute and Dallas Willard Center desires to support new resource and program development in the area of Christian spiritual formation. Part of these efforts will include the cultivation of a network of professional contacts through hosting and participating in conferences, and collaborating with other organizations that share the goals of the Martin Institute and Dallas Willard Center.